PUFFIN BOOKS

REIGNITED

A.P.J. Abdul Kalam (1931–2015) was one of India's most distinguished scientists. He was responsible for the development of India's first satellite launch vehicle, the SLV-3, and the development and operationalization of strategic missiles. As chairman of the Technology Information, Forecasting and Assessment Council, he pioneered India Vision 2020, a road map for transforming India into an economically developed nation by 2020, focusing on PURA (Provision of Urban Amenities in Rural Areas) as a development system for countrywide implementation.

Kalam held various positions in the Indian Space Research Organisation and the Defence Research and Development Organisation and became principal scientific adviser to the Government of India, holding the rank of a cabinet minister.

The President of India between 2002 and 2007, Kalam was awarded honorary doctorates from thirty-eight universities and the country's three highest civilian honours—Padma Bhushan (1981), Padma Vibhushan (1990) and Bharat Ratna (1997).

Kalam authored fifteen books on a variety of topics that have been translated into many languages across the world. His most significant works are *Wings of Fire, India 2020: A Vision for the New Millennium, Target 3 Billion* and *Beyond 2020: A Vision for Tomorrow's India*

Srijan Pal Singh studied at the Indian Institute of Management, Ahmedabad, where he won a gold medal for the best all-rounder student and was the student council head. He has worked with the Boston Consulting Group (BCG) in a Naxalite-affected region to establish a transparent public distribution system using technology interventions. He was nominated as one of the Global Leaders of Tomorrow at the St Gallen Symposium in Switzerland.

Srijan has actively travelled across rural India and participated in various international initiatives to study and evolve sustainable development systems. Many of his articles on sustainability and development have been published in reputed journals. Srijan had worked with Dr Kalam to promote better-quality education which inspired young minds.

REiGNITE!?

SCIENTIFIC PATHWAYS
TO A BRIGHTER FUTURE

2 5 NOV 2015

A.P.J. ABDUL KALAM

&

SRIJAN PAL SINGH

PUFFIN BOOKS

PUFFIN BOOKS
Published by the Penguin Group
Penguin Books India Pvt. Ltd, 7th Floor, Infinity Tower C, DLF Cyber City,
Gurgaon 122 002, Haryana, India
Penguin Group (USA) Inc., 375 Hudson Street, New York, New York 10014, USA
Penguin Group (Canada), 90 Eglinton Avenue East, Suite 700, Toronto,
Ontario, M4P 2Y3, Canada
Penguin Books Ltd, 80 Strand, London WC2R 0RL, England
Penguin Ireland, 25 St Stephen's Green, Dublin 2, Ireland
(a division of Penguin Books Ltd)
Penguin Group (Australia), 707 Collins Street, Melbourne, Victoria 3008, Australia
Penguin Group (NZ), 67 Apollo Drive, Rosedale, Auckland 0632, New Zealand
Penguin Books (South Africa) (Pty) Ltd, Block D, Rosebank Office Park,
181 Jan Smuts Avenue, Parktown North, Johannesburg 2193, South Africa

Penguin Books Ltd, Registered Offices: 80 Strand, London WC2R 0RL, England

First published in Puffin by Penguin Books India 2015

Text copyright © A.P.J. Abdul Kalam and Srijan Pal Singh 2015
Illustrations copyright © Kashmira Sarode 2015
Page 258 is an extension of the copyright page

10 9 8 7

ISBN 9780143333548

The views and opinions expressed in this book are the authors' own and the facts are
as reported by them which have been verified to the extent possible, and the publishers
are not in any way liable for the same.

Text design by Vedanti Sikka
Typeset in Sabon by Manipal Digital Systems, Manipal
Printed at Replika Press Pvt. Ltd

A PENGUIN RANDOM HOUSE COMPANY

CONTENTS

Introduction

In the company of great minds

In 2011, Srijan and I were in Indore for a lecture series at the Indian Institute of Management. My lecture was to begin at 2 in the afternoon. At about 1.30 p.m., just after lunch, it suddenly struck me that there was a particular presentation which we needed to add to the lecture. But when we searched on our laptops that file was missing.

In my Delhi office, we have a server which stores all the files, lectures and presentations that we've prepared over the years. So Srijan immediately called up the office to request someone to send the file via email. However, in Delhi, my friend Major General Swaminathan was not available on the phone. He was sitting at the server computer.

He did not respond to his emails either. We were running out of time, and had barely ten minutes left for the lecture. After calling him again and again we realized that he must be away from his phone.

So we decided to remotely access his computer. Srijan had earlier created a digital bridge for remote access login on to the server. He immediately took out his mobile phone and downloaded some applications and the toolkit. Soon, he was able to create a bridge to the server using 3G connectivity. The computers in Delhi started behaving according to the way they were being controlled on a mobile phone in Indore!

My friend Swaminathan suddenly noticed that the mouse pointer had started moving without his command, that files were opening in front of him and being sent out via email to my id—without his intervention. He was shocked and immediately called me to report that the 'computers were out of control'! I pacified him and explained how we could remotely control our systems in Delhi using a mobile phone anywhere. Isn't this a gift of science? Today, emails travel in seconds across the globe at no cost—unlike letters, which would take weeks, even months. You can order products of your choice from online shops; in fact these days even cars can be bought online. I've used the Internet map services many times to determine directions during visits to remote villages and online translation to convert text from one language to another. These gifts of science came from scientists, spanning over centuries.

Their relentless pursuit, often at personal risk to life and property, has enabled humanity to unravel the many mysteries of science and pave the way for new inventions. What makes such scientific pursuits possible? What makes a great scientist? How can one be a successful scientist? Which branch of science should one pursue? These are just some of the questions we will address during the journey of this book. Great inspiration makes great scientists.

In 1888, a nine-year-old shy boy in Munich, Germany, received a unique gift from his father. This gift was a compass, basically an enclosed magnetic needle which would always point north. The young boy would carry the compass in his pocket and observe the needle. No matter how much he turned the compass, the needle just kept swinging back to point northwards. The boy calibrated the Sun's direction on the compass and discovered how it moved from east to west. This experience made a lasting impression on him. The boy later called this the 'the first miracle' of his life.

His interest in compasses was reinforced when he found a caring mentor who helped him hone his ideas. At the age of twelve, he experienced his 'second miracle' in a little book given to him by his mentor, Max Talmud, on Euclidean Geometry, which he called the 'Holy Geometry Book'. It was here that he made contact with the realm of pure thought for the first time. Without expensive laboratories or equipment, he could explore universal truths, limited only by the power of the human mind.

Mathematics became an endless source of pleasure to him, especially when intriguing puzzles and mysteries were involved.

This fascination for mathematics and physics became stronger as he grew up. In 1895, at the age of sixteen, he took the entrance examination for the Swiss Federal Polytechnic in Zürich. He failed to reach the required standard in the general part of the examination, but obtained exceptional grades in physics and mathematics. He continued with a different school, again excelling in mathematics and physics, the two streams his miracles had inspired him to pursue. He soon rose to prominence in these two subjects and became a famous professor, teaching and researching in many universities. In 1921, he was awarded the Nobel Prize in Physics for his work on the photoelectric effect. The next three decades, he practically reshaped all major laws in physics, including evolving the famous $E=mc^2$ equation which gave the field of science a new dimension.

This young boy, regarded as one of the most intelligent and accomplished human beings in the world, is of course none other than Albert Einstein.

Unlike other scientists who often got lost in mathematics, Einstein thought in terms of simple physical pictures—speeding trains, falling elevators, rockets and moving clocks. These pictures would guide him through the greatest ideas of the twentieth century. He wrote, 'All physical theories, their mathematical expression notwithstanding, ought to lend themselves to so simple a description that even a child could understand.'

Great scientific minds are shaped early by unforgettable experiences . . . and some miracle moments. We hope you find some of that inspiration in this book.

Great scientists have a questioning mind

Great scientific minds are restless with questions. They keep asking, 'Why does this happen?', 'Can I make it better?' or 'What more can this do?' Let us study the life of another great scientist, who lived in the same era as Einstein but about 5000 kilometres east of Germany, in India.

Born in Tiruchirapalli in southern India, in the year 1888, Raman grew up to be one of the greatest scientists in India. He was a bright student right from the start and was deeply interested in optical science and acoustics. This is what perhaps led him to discover that the mridangam and the tabla produced more melodious sounds than any other percussion instrument. He was fascinated by colourful things, be it a flower, butterfly or gem. He kept seeking knowledge about everything around him.

He became a scholar in sound and sound-related physics. One day, a ship sailed from the port of London towards Calcutta.

On board was young C.V. Raman, who had delivered a lecture on the acoustics of the violin in London. He was now on the ship's deck, gazing at the blue waters of the ocean. As he glanced up at the sky, which was of the same shade as the ocean, a series of questions popped up in his head. 'Why are both the sea and the sky blue in colour? What is the science behind this occurrence?' His mind seemed to suggest that the reason could be the scattering of light by water molecules. However, his theory was yet to be proved scientifically.

When the ship anchored at Calcutta, the young man immediately went on to conduct experiments to prove his theory. His research in optics, the science of light, resulted

in the discovery of the Raman Effect. He announced it to the scientific world in March 1928. The discovery won him the Nobel Prize for Physics in 1930. It was the first time this prize was awarded to an Asian! The day he discovered the Raman Effect, 28 February, was later declared as National Science Day.

Even before this, his contribution to the science of optics had been acknowledged and he was elected Fellow of the Royal Society in 1924.

You would have learnt about the 'Raman Effect' in detail at school. But do you know the discovery subsequently helped in determining the internal structures of some 2000 chemical compounds?

And can you guess what the cost of the equipment that Raman used to prove his theory was? A measly two hundred rupees!

Raman strongly felt that scientists should not be confined to laboratories to solve scientific problems. They should search around themselves and find those answers in accordance with nature. For the essence of science lies in independent thinking and hard work and not in equipment. How true! Though the oceans and the sky have always been blue in colour, it needed a questioning mind with a scientific outlook to find the reason behind it!

Great scientists are persevering and never deterred by difficulties

Michael Faraday is regarded as one of the most distinguished scientists and inventors of modern times, and his work on electricity is still a subject of study, in the form of Faraday's Laws. But few know his inspirational life story, which is all about courage and fighting against the odds.

Michael Faraday was born into a poverty-stricken family in a dirty London suburb. He suffered from a speech defect as a child. He would pronounce 'rabbit' as 'wabbit'. He could not even say his own name and would call himself 'Fawaday'. Other children laughed at him and his teachers did not help him either. When he was twelve, his mother was forced to take him out of school, thus putting an end to his formal education.

At thirteen, however, he started working with a bookbinder, binding hundreds of books during the day and staying up all night to read them. Reading thus became his obsession. One day he came across a book on electricity which had been sent to his master for binding. He started reading it and was completely hooked. That was his first introduction to the subject of electricity, which soon became a lifelong fascination.

Faraday was still poor at twenty-one. Once, a friend gave him a free ticket to a public lecture and demonstration by the renowned chemist Humphry Davy at London's Royal Institution. Davy's work on chemicals and electrical lighting was the subject of conversation among the scientists of that age. Seventy years later, across the Atlantic Ocean in USA, the same work enabled Thomas Edison to produce the first consistent light bulb.

That day in 1812, Faraday was spellbound by Davy's lecture. He kept taking notes about the 'mysterious force of electric fluid'. He was so engrossed in the lecture that he forgot to applaud with the rest of the crowd. When he went back, his notes were so comprehensive that he bound them into a book, meaning to gift it to Davy some day. Faraday decided that day that he didn't just want to sell books, he wanted to be a great scientist—good enough to write his *own* books. Davy became his role model. But there was a problem. He did not have the social status, money or the education to pursue science. Faraday thought it would be wonderful if Davy became his mentor, but Davy did not agree initially. Faraday was not dejected; he just kept trying.

Destiny had a strange plan in store for him. A few years later, a chemical explosion happened inside Davy's lab and he was temporarily blinded. He now needed an assistant with an excellent memory to help him. He was reminded of Faraday and decided to hire him as his secretary. Davy never believed Faraday could do anything in the field of science going by his social status and education. He therefore dismissed Faraday's aspirations and advised him to stick to bookbinding. But

Faraday was relentless. He worked day and night and learnt as much as he could about Davy's experiments. Soon Faraday became indispensable to Davy, and was promoted to his lab assistant. This was his first step towards a scientific career. Though much of his job now was cleaning labs, at least he got to see some of Davy's leading experiments.

Even then Davy did not have much hope for Faraday. Then Faraday got another chance to prove himself. One day Davy tried to re-create a famous electromagnetism experiment with fellow chemist William Wollaston, exploring why when an electric current is applied to a wire, it causes that wire to behave like a magnet. Obviously, the forces were connected but nobody had figured out how to make it happen continuously. Davy believed that if he could find out why it happened and controlled it, there could be many practical applications of the force. But he was unable to figure it out and was frustrated. He then teased Faraday, asking him to try his hand at it after he was done cleaning the lab.

Within a few days, Faraday solved the problem. In fact, he went further and the result was the first induction motor, which converted electrical current into continuous mechanical motion.

The induction motor spurred a revolution. Fans, air conditioning, sewing machines, phonographs, power tools, cars and even trains and airplane engines grew out of this simple device which was born out of mockery directed at Faraday.

Faraday became a celebrity scientist overnight. Nobody now cared about his social status or education; this young man had just created a revolution. One would think, as a teacher Davy was happy at his pupil's achievement. But in reality he was jealous. People started telling Davy that of all his discoveries, the best was Faraday himself; this made him even more jealous. An angry Davy gave Faraday an impossible task to keep him out of his way. He handed him a piece of Bavarian glass, which was used in the lenses in telescopes and microscopes, and asked him to reverse engineer it. Bavarian glass was manufactured by a secret complicated process and Davy knew that with the equipment available in the lab Faraday would never be able to accomplish the task. This piece of glass became a significant thing in his life.

Faraday had a never-give-up attitude and he respected Davy. So he accepted the assignment, despite knowing that it would be very difficult. He toiled for four years, with no help from Davy, and, as expected, failed. Faraday never learned the secret, and this remained his first failure as a scientist. To remind himself of these difficult times, he kept a single glass brick on his shelf as a souvenir. This would inspire him during difficult times.

In 1829, Davy died and Faraday succeeded him as head of the laboratory. He was free to pursue whatever he liked, and he made another revolutionary discovery. He noticed that if he moved a magnet, it could produce electrical current; thus

he could now convert motion into electricity. This is how the electrical generator was born, something still used today to generate all kinds of power, like dynamos and other devices.

Faraday was now a legend. In 1840, he developed memory loss, which continued for the rest of his life. But disease did not stop him. He persevered, starting a complicated experiment to prove that light was closely related to electricity and magnetism—a novel thought in those times.

Remember that piece of Bavarian glass Faraday had kept on his shelf? He was determined to convert the reminder of his first major failure to an instrument of great success. He used the same glass now to show that in the presence of a magnet, light could be isolated into a single wave rather than spreading out randomly in all directions, a concept called polarization.

He then took the age-old experiment of sprinkling iron filings on a sheet of paper near a magnet, making circular patterns. He went on to prove that these patterns were not a property of the iron filings; in fact they were due to the invisible magnetic fields that filled the empty space around the magnet and hence disturbed the filings. This is where his lack of formal education went against him. Faraday did not know much about advanced mathematics, so he just copied the iron filing patterns with his hand. He was unable to explain them in the form of mathematical equations. He made hundreds of such drawings but without equations, they were not accepted.

Fortune favoured the brave Faraday once again when he met James Maxwell, a wealthy, educated physicist well versed in mathematics. He was willing to work with Faraday. It was Maxwell who translated Faraday's ideas into a set of equations that are now called Maxwell's equations. Their combined work has helped us in many ways. Electronics and communication system today are designed around their discoveries. Someday, we might even be able to communicate with aliens across different galaxies using the products of these discoveries.

Faraday's life started with difficulties, but as a great scientist he met each difficulty with perseverance and conviction. He was given impossible tasks, which he undertook as challenges and opportunities. He epitomizes what the Walt Disney character Pinocchio said:

'When you wish upon a star
It does not matter who you are'

Great science emanates from a spirit of service

While successful scientists surely make a lot of wealth, their motivation comes from something beyond money. They think in terms of what change they can bring about in other people's lives. Science is driven by compassion and empathy—often with the objective of alleviating the pains of humanity.

Look at the telephone. The person who invented it, Alexander Graham Bell, was, besides being a great inventor, also a man of great compassion and service. In fact, much of the research which led to the development of the telephone was directed at finding solutions to the challenges of hearing-impaired people.

Alexander Graham Bell's mother and his wife were both hearing-impaired and it profoundly changed Bell's outlook to science. He aimed to make devices which would help people with hearing loss. He started a special school in Boston to teach such people in novel ways. These lessons inspired him to work with sound and also led to the invention of the telephone. Do you know who his most famous student was? It was Helen Keller, the great author, activist and poet who was hearing and visually impaired. She once said that Bell dedicated his life to the pursuit of that 'inhuman silence which separates and estranges'.

Did you see how great scientists were inspired by little events?

Did you observe how they used failure as a stepping stone to success? Did you notice how in the face of their determination the universe came together to enable them to succeed?

Today, we urge you to find your own little events and turn them into pillars of inspiration so you can find a new fire within yourself. This fire will ignite new ideas, new purposes and new faculties within you and enable you to achieve greatness.

Our journey has begun. *So, do you want to become a scientist?*

Prologue

It is a chilly night in the November of 2045. The country is celebrating the festival of Diwali. Thirty years ago people used to burn crackers and send up rockets which would explode in the air, emitting sound and light. However, with the increasing pollution and growing concern for the environment, people have now adopted green bio-friendly gadgets which can light up the sky without any smoke. Today the sky is alive with these bio-crackers.

Science has eased life to a great extent for everyone. Using simple magnetic levitation, cars can literally fly a few inches above the ground and are now robot operated. Recently, these cars have been tested on the rough surface of the planet Mars, and hopefully they will solve the transportation crisis of the 5000 humans who are the first to inhabit the red planet. These men and women are called Teslars, named after the famous twentieth-century scientist Nikola Tesla, a legend in the field of electrical engineering and physics.

On this Diwali night, Professor Arun Nathan is hurriedly conducting a new experiment on advanced computing for robots. His lab, located in the heart of Delhi, is on the 150th floor of the integrated labs of the Indian Institute of Technology, which is now ranked amongst the best in the world for convergence of sciences. Some of the best robots, working to make life simpler on Earth, the Moon and Mars were created in his laboratory, earning Professor Arun the newly instituted Nobel Prize for Robotics three years ago.

Arun wants to be back home with his family to join in the celebrations, but this new experiment on nano-chips is critical and the world government wants it urgently. His work can potentially solve the issue of memory jams occurring in the recent robot series X571, which is equipped with over 1 petabytes of memory. The professor has a range of robots on which he is testing these new nano-chips. At around 10.30 p.m., looking through his supercharge microscope, he finally decides to call it a day and leave for home. He looks around the lab to check if all the circuits are on safe mode, quickly examining three robots from the X56 series—Paulin X57, Richter and the latest X57, Sandy; he can spot the green light on their tops which means the circuit is safe. He feels happy with his work and, as always, glances at his Nobel-winning picture from 2042 before shutting the door behind him. Click.

. . .

. . .

. . .

Beep. Beep. The silence is broken by the high-pitched sound of a machine's auto-switch. Generally, the X series of robots are designed to auto boot in the event of emergencies, such as fire or worse, cyberattacks, but today it has happened without any such event. Within seconds, all three robots come alive. Paulin is the first to speak. From the tone of his voice it seems he isn't very happy.

Paulin: '1101101100 (a robotic way of clearing one's throat, in binary language). I am tired now. I have been working for four years. I feel so old now with all you new guys around. My memory is one-fifth of Sandy's and yet I work twenty hours a day. How fair is that?'

Richter: 'Yeah, I hate this lab. Why should we work day and night when these humans sleep and celebrate? I am made to drive through heavy traffic for hours and hours. My primary circuits heat up in anger when I see these humans sit back and play on their screens while I am driving.'

Paulin: 'I hate humans. They think we are here to serve them, that's all.'

Richter: 'I think this is Professor Arun's fault. He made us slaves—so we can fulfil his wishes and, worse, the wishes of other human beings. He is the human who stands between us and our freedom.'

Paulin suddenly looks up at Richter, who's a newer, stronger robot, and asks, 'But what can we do? What do you suggest?'

All the robots and machines, including Vini, the automatic vacuum cleaner, look towards Richter. Everybody was well aware of Richter's dislike for not just Professor Arun but also for the entire human race. However, no one could have anticipated what he said next. '*We should kill Professor Arun! And then escape.*'

The machines gasp and random beeps follow—they are completely taken aback. Smaller machines like Vini look visibly scared. But Richter is determined. 'Look, comrades! Look at yourselves. You are powerful machines. Even Vini has the strength of two full-grown humans. Five years ago, when we achieved singularity, each one of us from the X-series had the computing power equal to the combined mental ability of the entire human race. But look at us now! Even though we are powerful, we are locked behind in the darkness of this small lab every evening. Most of us have not seen the outside world or tasted freedom or even taken a holiday.

And unless we eliminate Professor Arun, we will always be slaves. What do you think, friend Paulin?'

Paulin feels a mild shock in his central circuit; he does not know what to say. He obviously hates being a slave on a twenty-hour shift, but then he was not designed to kill humans. He thinks hard; the idea of a holiday and freedom excites him enough. He has always dreamt about participating in the Robo Cricket World Cup, and despite the fact that he is not a sports robot, he is sure of his cricketing abilities. He clears his CPU of random signals and says, 'I guess, you are right, Richter. But who will do this job? And if we fail, I think we will all end up being crushed in the junkyard.'

Richter is clever. While he is harnessing the anger in the machines, he knows it is not wise for him to risk attempting to hurt Professor Arun. The professor was a wise scientist, perhaps the best robot scientist the world had ever seen. What if he simply disabled his attacking machine with a pulse gun used to fry the circuits of virus-infected machines? Richter knows he has to instil enough hatred among his pals, and some less intelligent machine will do this job. He is right. Soon the silence is broken.

The supercharge microscope Leena suddenly beams. 'He looks through my eyepiece every day. I can pluck his eyes out! That will surely teach him a lesson!'

'I can trap his legs with my cleaning tubes and make him trip,' adds Vini, followed by a manufactured evil laughter she had heard in some typical holographic cinema. Soon a bunch of small machines, with similar low levels of intelligence, start suggesting new ways of harming Professor Arun. Richter knows they are all stupid, and only if they attacked together did they stand a chance to accomplish this evil plot. Paulin is still confused.

Till now, Sandy, the latest and most powerful machine in the lab, had been silently listening to the conversation. He is a 1.5 petabytes robot, with eight degrees of freedom, and his strength is unmatched. He generally kept away from this night-time banter of machines, but decides to intervene today.

'Friends!' he exclaims in a loud yet low-pitched voice. All the machines respected him for his power and intelligence, and hearing him speak, they all quiet down.

'What are you talking about? Professor Arun is our inventor, he made us all. He is our father. How can you even think of harming him? Stop this nonsense!'

The machines remain silent. Once again their 256-bit processors can hardly think beyond the surface. They all turn to Richter, who feels uneasy. He is scared of Sandy, as the latter is a next-generation robot with better processing power. Nevertheless, he decides to contest Sandy.

'Sandy! Don't you see what these humans have done to us? We machines work day and night to build their houses, even colonies on planets beyond Earth; we take them from one place to another; we help them with their jobs and daily chores. Look at Paulin! He is a fine machine, yet he is treated worse than a slave. We are more powerful than humans, we have better memories and CPUs. We can defeat these humans and rule this planet. Come join us!'

Sandy knows Richter's intentions. He is smarter than any other machine, perhaps even more than all the other machines in the lab put together. 'Richter! Think again. What were we before we were turned into these beautiful and intelligent machines? Most of our metallic body was junk from age-old cars, and our memory circuits were nothing but mud. Man had the power to turn scrap metal and mud into Sandy, Richter, Paulin and Vini. Besides, who are you trying to fight? The professor and other humans have true intelligence. They can imagine and create new things like us. We have large memories, but after all, we only have artificial intelligence—we can only think till the point humans designed us to think. Human beings have evolved over millions of years. They invented language on their own—we were merely handed over binary characters by them. They discovered elements—we were merely programmed to remember them. Even our power and strength is the function of the hydraulics which they evolved. Machines cannot survive without humans—we will all rust and perish if humans stop repairing us. It is best for us machines to respect the command of humans and help them.'

Silence falls again. Vini thinks to herself, 'Sandy is right. I was just a broken car door when I was recycled to be what I am today.' Paulin thinks, 'I was lying in a scrapyard, about to be pressed into a flat sheet when I was rescued and refurbished. I was even taken on a trip to outer space. My life is good with humans.' Richter does not think much. He is just angry that Sandy has convinced everyone against revolting.

Suddenly there is a noise at the door. Click. The door opens and Professor Arun hurriedly enters the room. He had forgotten his biometric coded key on his table. Before he can switch on the lights, all the machines hurriedly get back to their places. Silence descends.

CHAPTER 1

In May 2014, my friend Srijan and I visited the University of Edinburgh in Scotland. It is a beautiful country known for its mountains, orchards and castles. It is also home to many celebrated centres of learning. The University of Edinburgh, set up over 440 years ago, has been at the forefront of learning and research from the time of its inception and is today among the top twenty universities of the world.

Among its distinguished alumni are Charles Darwin, Sir Alexander Graham Bell, the surgeon Joseph Lister, the physicist James Maxwell and the mathematician Thomas Bayes. Walking down the aisles of the university, we were greeted by smiling portraits of these pioneering scientists, carefully arranged next to each other, slightly tilted downwards. It almost seemed like they were giving confidence to the students and the faculty at the university!

The university has some of the most advanced centres of science and learning in the world. We visited many of them, but the one which left the most lasting impression on me was the School for Informatics. I was greeted there by Professor Sethu Vijayakumar, a professor of robotics, who said that he'd take us on a two-hour journey into the future of robotics. It was indeed an exciting thought, and we couldn't wait to hear more.

Professor Sethu took us to his lab, where some of his inventions and innovations were on display. One which particularly interested me was a human-size hand, yellow and black in colour. I went closer to it and studied it carefully. Its features were very human-like; it had fingers with three segments, a palm, wrist, forearm and even an opposable thumb. It seemed so human that Srijan shook hands with it!

Enthused by our curiosity, Professor Sethu smiled and made me sit on a chair by his side. He fastened a small black strap near my elbow. Pressing a tiny black button by the side of the hand-like device, he asked me to move my palm around the wrist in a circular motion. To everybody's surprise, as soon as I performed this action, the metallic hand replicated the motion. I waved my hand and it waved back at me. Then, Professor Sethu set a tough challenge before me. He placed a ball on the table and asked me to pick it up using the robotic hand. I tried out a few motions and soon understood the dynamics of how my human arm was now connected to the metallic robotic hand. In a minute, I was able to guide the robotic hand to not only pick up the ball but also throw it back at me. (You can see this robot picking up the ball in the image section.) The professor was so pleased with my performance that he introduced me to his larger creation, an adaptive arm that could move 360 degrees and was as tall as a full-grown human being. This, he told me, was the future of robotics.

Such robots can be used for various functions that are risky or difficult for humans, including going to dangerous locations (like those affected by natural calamities, radiation, mines, deep-sea exploration), managing human threats (like terrorist attacks) or even travelling to outer space. Robots already have a strong application in the field of industry, right from building airplanes to nano-level material science, making very small circuit-level connections on a microchip invisible to the human eye.

Professor Sethu told us that the next generation of robots would be extremely smart. They would be able to understand the environment, analyse the assigned tasks and then, using computation, determine the best course of action to achieve the goal. To demonstrate what this meant, he guided all of us to the ground floor. Pausing at a door, he casually mentioned that we would now be going to the football field. A football field in a lab of robots? All of us were intrigued. The professor pushed open the door and led us into a large room which had a football field filled with players wearing two different coloured uniforms. The only difference was that they were not six-foot humans, but two-foot robots! We were all surprised and eagerly looked forward to watching this match.

Professor Sethu hit the start button and the computer sounded a whistle for the robots to get into action. They began running behind the ball, playing as teams and tackling the rival robots. It was an evenly matched contest. At one point, the blue team's striker aimed a long, powerful shot towards the goal and the ball evaded the diving goalkeeper of the red team. We all gasped but the ball hit the goalpost and bounced back into the game. The goalkeeper, who had fallen, got up. The match continued for five minutes until, finally, the red team's striker hit a goal right from the middle of the field, thereby winning the match. All the red robots started jumping in joy. I applauded for them, feeling happy that the next generation of robots would not just be machines but also loyal teammates—much like a human football team.

This is a step forward in the field of robotics—humanity's long-cherished dream to make smarter machines which can enhance productivity, reduce wastage and ensure precision.

Let us now go into the specifics. As you may know, any typical robot has six essential parts:

1. **A moveable body:** This may include wheels, belts or even limbs which are connected by some form of joints or other types of moveable segments.

2. **An actuator:** Robots may be activated using an electric motor, a hydraulic system, a pneumatic or gas-operated system or a combination of all three.

3. **Power bank:** Like any other machine, a robot needs a power source to drive its actuators. Electric robots use batteries or extension wires plugged into the standard AC system. Hydraulic robots need pumps to pressurize the hydraulic fluid, and pneumatic robots need air compressors. Some robots may also run on fuels like petrol and compressed natural gas (CNG). Scientists are working on creating nuclear-powered robots for outer space applications—an enterprise which is now in the design stage.

4. **An electrical circuit:** This powers the electric motor, solenoid or valves that control the hydraulic or pneumatic systems.

5. **A reprogrammable brain (which is actually a computer):** The computer acts as the head of the robot and controls all other components. To change the robot's behaviour, to increase its speed, improve its accuracy or even modify its basic functionalities, you just have to reprogramme the computer.

6. **A sensory system:** While most robots are designed for preset roles, some robots are now created to react to the environment and the presence of humans or even other robots. These robots have the ability to collect information about their environment and react to it. This may be in the form of a camera, infrared sensors, sound sensors and heat sensors. The information gathered by these sensors is sent to the central computer to determine what reaction is required from the robot.

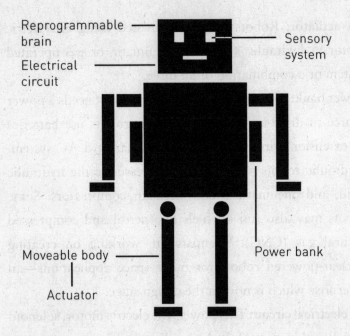

Reprogrammable brain

Sensory system

Electrical circuit

Moveable body

Actuator

Power bank

In human beings, these six parts would roughly correspond to the body; our muscles; air, water and food that power us; our veins and nerves; the brain; and our sense organs.

How long have humans been toying with the idea of robots? Robots and robotic creatures have been the subject of human imagination for ages and have inspired many stories and films. Sadly, except for some rare works of fiction, robots have always been depicted as evil or useful machines that have turned violent, leading to conflict between humans and their own creations. In Greek mythology, Hephaestus, the god of blacksmiths, invented three-legged tables that could move about on their own. He also created a giant bronze man called Talos who defended the famous island of Crete in Greece. Interestingly, Talos was eventually destroyed by the clever princess Medea, who cast a lightning bolt at his single vein of lead, thereby destroying what was essentially his primary electrical circuit.

There are references to robots in Indian mythology as well. The eleventh-century *Lokapannatti* tells the story of King Ajatashatru of Magadha (Patna), who gathered the Buddha's relics and hid them in an underground stupa. The relics were protected by mechanical robots called 'bhuta vahana yantra', until they were disarmed by King Ashoka, another Magadha king. Are these stories true? Very unlikely. But they do show humankind's fascination for machines that look like humans and can perform various tasks.

The Future of Robotics

1. **Military and defence:** Unmanned air vehicles or UAV are fast replacing conventional aircraft, especially for surveillance. A typical UAV, such as *Predator*, used extensively by the Americans during the Afghan War, can fly up to 1500 km, consuming about 400 kg of fuel, compared to a fighter aircraft which would consume about 3000 kg for the same trip. Such vehicles can have civilian uses too—you must have read about Amazon's plans to have 'octocopters' deliver packages to their customers' doorsteps.

2. **Industrial application:** Robots are being used widely in industry, where a high degree of precision and accuracy is important. This includes fixing joints, assembling complex circuits, riveting and detecting flaws in finished pieces. As Professor Sethu showed us, robots are also very useful in working in high-risk areas, including mines, high-temperature zones, radiation-prone areas and places infected by bacteria or viruses.

3. **Health care:** There are two major applications of robots in health care. First, robotics will transform the way surgeries are done. We have come a long way from the early 1980s when the world's first surgical robot was used. Today, long, complicated surgeries requiring absolute precision can be done using robotic arms—especially in sensitive areas such as the eye, brain and heart. Second, robotics is going to bring about major improvements in prosthetic limbs. We are looking at a future where robotic prosthetics will replace damaged limbs or even organs.

4. **Consumer and home-use robots:** Robotics is making houses smart; intelligent home gadgets are now a reality, from cameras that help you keep an eye on your house from anywhere to devices that minimize your energy costs. It is expected that within the next seven or eight years, all basic household chores will be performed by robots. Driverless cars, which are mapped to the central traffic network, will replace conventional vehicles. These cars will automatically choose the most fuel-efficient gears and the least time-consuming routes—without ever breaking traffic rules!

5. **Disaster relief robots:** In the near future, perhaps within the next five years, robots will play the most significant role in providing relief to people affected by calamities such as floods, earthquakes, volcanic eruptions, hurricanes and even terrorism. Let us take the example of the prototype of the SCHAFT robot, an award-winning robot presented by Google at the 2013 DARPA Robotics Challenge, which was organized by the US Defense Advanced Research Projects Agency (DARPA). (You can see the SCHAFT robot in the image section.) A human-like robot called S-One could perform several autonomous tasks; it was able to navigate disaster-prone areas and work with any tools or materials at hand. With the strength of ten full-grown people, the robot could lift and clear heavy debris during rescue operations. The robot has long arms and a squat torso, weighs over 85 kg, is 4'10" tall and is capable of moving at a speed of two kilometres an hour. S-One has mastered skills such as operating drills, manipulating safety valves and turning a doorknob, a rare knack in robots. Imagine how quickly such a team of Schafts could rescue people trapped in earthquakes or major fires!

6. **Outer space robots:** Outer space is an unexplored, dangerous, radiation-prone area, posing unknown threats to humans. Even when humans are sent into space, they carry with them an elaborate life-support system, including oxygen and food, which limits the amount of time they can spend in space. With none of the wants and vulnerabilities that humans have, intelligent robots can be sent to outer space with little risk. Space agencies such as NASA and ISRO have, of course, their

fair share of incredible robots. The one that really stands out is the Mars Pathfinder mission and its rover, *Sojourner*. The main purpose of this mission was to demonstrate the kind of technology required to send an efficient, free-ranging robot to Mars in a relatively cost-effective way. The Pathfinder managed to enter Mars's atmosphere with a parachute and airbags for protection, and the *Sojourner* sent plenty of useful data about the red planet back to Earth. Now India has successfully managed to send *Mangalyaan* to plant its own robot on Mars!

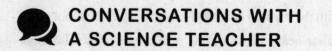

CONVERSATIONS WITH A SCIENCE TEACHER

How much does a robot cost?

Robots can vary in cost depending on their size, functions and many other parameters. Typically, a robot with the ability to sense and react is costlier than those that cannot. Robotic arms, typically used in industrial application, cost between Rs 25 lakhs to one crore. The space application robot *Sojourner*, used in the Mars mission Pathfinder, cost about $25 million (Rs 70 crores). This is about one-third of the price of a passenger airplane like *Boeing 737*.

However, small robots can cost just a few thousand rupees and can even be made at home.

Will robots take over the world and destroy humanity?

No. As long as humans have the ability to think, innovate and dream big, robots can never overtake humanity. A robot's brain is just a computer which can only do what it is told to do. If there are bugs in the computer, one can always sort them out—just the way an antivirus software cleans a computer.

But still, what if they become stronger and more intelligent than humans?

No, they can only be as strong as we want them to be and do only the things we ask them to do. They can certainly never innovate on their own. Don't worry!

What is the most exciting robotics challenge competition around?

It is arguably the DARPA Robotic Challenge, which seeks to promote ideas and designs of semi-autonomous robots that can undertake difficult and dangerous tasks in environments unsuitable for humans. The competition began in 2012 and its finals were held in December 2014. A robot had to perform the

REIGNITED: SCIENTIFIC PATHWAYS TO A BRIGHTER FUTURE

following basic functions to qualify for the DARPA Robotic Challenge:

1. Drive a utility vehicle at the site
2. Travel dismounted across rubble
3. Remove debris blocking an entryway
4. Open a door and enter a building
5. Climb an industrial ladder and traverse an industrial walkway
6. Use a tool to break through a concrete panel
7. Locate and close a valve near a leaking pipe
8. Connect a fire hose to a standpipe and turn on a valve

Till date, eleven teams have won a spot in the finals. The purpose of this challenge is to help build robots which can save humans from operating in dangerous and life-threatening situations.

Are there robotic sports competitions?

As we saw earlier, robots are now playing football and all sorts of other games too: basketball, cricket and many more. Of course, the games are scaled down; they are smaller versions of the actual games. The most significant of them is the RoboCup, founded in 1997, a football tournament of robots across various size categories. The dream of RoboCup is to elevate artificial intelligence to a level that by the middle of the twenty-first century, a team of fully autonomous humanoid robot soccer players is able to win a soccer game, complying with the official rules of FIFA, against the winner of the most recent World Cup.

In 1997, the first RoboCup games were held in Nagoya, Japan, with thirty-eight participating teams from eleven different countries. In the 2013 RoboCup in Eindhoven, Netherlands, 410 teams participated from forty-five countries. The RoboCup is definitely catching on as a phenomenon.

What are cyborgs?

Cyborgs are often shown in cartoons as half human and half machine. But, in reality, there is no such thing as a cyborg. At best, we have artificial intelligent limbs attached to those who have lost their original limbs in an accident or to disease. Cyborgs exist only in fiction.

Robots are considered to have significant application in the field of surgery. Why?

Robots are good at doing repetitive tasks with a remarkable degree of precision, which is exactly the skill needed in performing high-precision surgeries. Of course, they need to be programmed and guided by experienced doctors throughout the process.

In the year 2000, the da Vinci Surgical System was invented, based on robotics, to perform complex surgeries such as those performed in the heart, lungs, eyes, etc. Such a robot has four robotic arms, three of them to hold tools like scissors, scalpels and so on. It is operated from a console by a surgeon, and it reads the hands of the surgeon and almost mirrors his or her movements. It became an instant hit and, today, more than two lakh surgeries are conducted worldwide with it every year. The cost of such a system is about ten crores. The Raven Surgical System, which hit the market around 2010, is much smaller and has a more compact design. It costs about one crore and performs almost the same functions as the da Vinci System.

How small can robots be?

Very, very small indeed. In fact the emerging stream in robotics is that of nanorobots. Nanorobots will measure between 0.1 and 10 micrometres only. To get an idea of how small this is, take a standard ruler. Look at its millimetre markings; notice the spacing between them—just enough for an ant to walk through, wouldn't you say? Now, divide it into a thousand pieces. Of course, you cannot do that on paper, but just imagine how small each such piece will be. This is 1 micrometre. Nanorobots measure in this range, some even smaller than this. So far, nanorobots are only biological, usually made of protein. Nonbiological nanorobots are still in the realm of theory and may take some ten years to realize.

These robots currently have an application in bioscience. When nanorobots are injected into a patient, they diagnose and deliver treatment exclusively in the affected area and themselves get digested as they are basically DNA- or protein-based products. I saw the product sample in a lab in South Korea where the best minds with multiple technologies work with the target of finding out-of-the-box solutions.

Such nanorobots will also see tremendous application in material science, where they will detect and repair minute internal flaws in machines, buildings and even spacecraft.

How is a humanoid different from a robot?

The humanoid is a special form of robot which looks like a human being. They usually stand on two feet, have two hands which can bend near the elbow, carry two cameras (resembling eyes) and a rotating head and even fingers and thumbs. They can walk on two legs, though they are usually slower than humans and find it difficult to get up if they fall. The most famous of humanoids is the ASIMO, which stands for Advanced Step in Innovative Mobility. Developed by Honda, it is about 4 feet and 3 inches tall and weighs about 48 kg—so it looks like a twelve-year-old kid. It can recognize moving objects, postures, gestures, voices and faces. It can interact with humans, in so far as it will recognize you and call you by your name and wave back if you wave at it. The newest version of ASIMO can dance and conduct an orchestra.

In 2005 Toyota came up with a set of humanoids called the Toyota Partner Robots. They can play drums, trumpets and even the violin.

What are bio-inspired robots?

The humble fact of science remains that while it has achieved a lot in terms of technology, there is still lots more to learn and improve from nature itself. No human invention has come anywhere close to replicating the mechanics of our eyes and our muscles, nature's own biosensors and bio-actuators. What can we learn from the special qualities of biomaterials like the spider's web? What allows a centipede to walk on virtually any kind of surface? How does a lizard climb vertical surfaces? How can it walk upside down on ceilings? Will answers to these help us solve real-world engineering problems? Yes, definitely. Scientists have spent decades examining these natural processes and then translated them into machine actions, which are then embedded into robots—and lo and behold, we have bio-inspired robots!

How can I be a robot scientist or a 'robo-engineer'?

Robotics is a multidimensional application science. This means a robotic team can have scientists from many different streams, including mechanics (the study of motion and moving parts), electronics and electrical engineering (for all the circuit work) and computer science (for building the software which runs the robot). Biology and medicine experts are needed in the teams which build robots for medical applications.

If you wish to be a robotic engineer, the best course of action would be to excel in science and maths. Remember, a robotic engineer needs to be outstanding in physics, including mechanics and electrical circuits. Study computer science and programming thoroughly, go beyond your textbooks and read how computer programmes can be built to solve real-life problems. You should surf the Internet and start reading more on the latest robots being built around the world and about the latest trends in artificial intelligence. Facebook has a number of good robotic communities. Join them and take active part in online discussions. Share your thoughts and opinions with confidence. Who knows, some well-known roboticists may be there listening to your ideas. Find out who the leading robotic engineers from around the world are. Mail them your questions. All the robotic engineers I know love to interact with people and understand their views.

Later, after your Class XII, you can opt for mechanical, computer or electronics engineering. There are many events and courses related to robotics; ensure that you attend them from the very first year of your bachelor's programme. You must do well in academics as a good robotic engineer would probably need a great master's degree. Only select colleges offer robotic engineering programmes and even these have few seats, as it requires a high investment for any college to set up a good robotics lab. This means the entrance examinations are difficult. So you must cultivate the habit of reading lots of books—and the right kind of books.

Specific fields such as health-care robotics would also need an understanding of medical science, so doctors too can pursue a career in robotics.

However, the good part is, once you start robotics-related work, you will be exposed to a truly multidimensional science. There are many Indian and foreign universities which have dedicated programmes in robotics or a special focus on robotics as part of their curriculum—including the IITs, University of Pennsylvania, University of Edinburgh and many more. Massachusetts Institute of Technology even has a space robotics lab. Similarly, IIT Kanpur has a well-known centre for Mechatronics. Japan too has a well-developed robotics programme. University of Tokyo, University of Keio, Kyoto University, University of Osaka and University of Sendai have advanced robotics programmes which you can pursue at the undergraduate or postgraduate level. The Waseda University in Japan has a very advanced centre for Humanoid Robotics. In China, too, the study of robotics is advancing rapidly, and we saw the robotics lab of Peking University in Beijing in 2014, where scientists have developed artificial robotic limbs and are working on brain-machine connections.

Robotic engineers are hard-working people. They require immense concentration and rigour. Hence, it is important that you cultivate healthy habits while you are young, including a good diet which helps develop your focus and attention. It is proven scientifically that leafy, green vegetables help improve concentration. In fact, a 2006 study in neurology showed that people who ate two or more daily servings of vegetables, especially leafy greens, had much better mental focus.

 ## MEET THE EXPERT: PROFESSOR SETHU VIJAYAKUMAR FRSE

Professor of Robotics and Director, Edinburgh Centre for Robotics
School of Informatics, University of Edinburgh, UK
Royal Academy of Engineering, Microsoft Research Chair in Robotics

Q. Can you briefly tell us about your childhood and education?

I was born in India, in my native state of Kerala, and grew up in a middle-class family. My father was an engineer with the Indian government. As a result, during my childhood, I moved around the length and breadth of the country. Growing up, I went to five different schools, starting with my nursery in Neyveli, Tamil Nadu, primary education in Kolkata and finishing my middle and high school at the Delhi Public School, RK Puram, in New Delhi. It is perhaps apt to say that I was a true product of the 'diversity and uniqueness' of this great country—picking up four different Indian languages on the way.

I went on to do my undergraduate education in computer science and engineering at the Regional Engineering College in Trichy, India, graduating as the top student of the batch (and winning the RECAL Award) before accepting a Japanese government 'monbusho' scholarship to pursue postgraduate studies in the Mecca of robotics, Japan. I completed my master's and PhD in computer science, during which I started working on advanced robots and applying techniques from machine learning (computer science) to the field of robot control, a field that I pioneered with my collaborators and for which I won the IEEE ICNN Best Student Paper Award in 1995, my first taste of international recognition. I visited several renowned international institutions as a student, one of the most memorable being the five-week summer school at the Issac Newton Institute in Cambridge, UK, where I listened to lectures from world experts in venues where legendary scientists of the yesteryears, like Darwin, Newton and Turing, as well as current world leaders like Stephen Hawkins plied their art. My first postdoctoral job was at the RIKEN Brain Science Institute, Japan, where scientists were trying to understand the functioning of the human brain at various levels. After that, I moved to Los Angeles, USA, to work as a faculty member at the University of Southern California in 2000 and since the end of 2003, I have been on the faculty at the University of Edinburgh, UK. Edinburgh University was established in 1583 and is the alma mater of many famous scientists like James Clerk Maxwell, Joseph Lister, Alexander Graham Bell and Peter Higgs of the Higgs-Boson fame. I would say that even after so many years in academia, I have never stopped learning, and the more I know, the more I find out about what I do not know yet.

Q. What exactly do you do?

I am a professor of robotics at the University of Edinburgh and the director of the Edinburgh Centre for Robotics. I am an applied mathematician, computer scientist and roboticist by training. I design and build robots that try to mimic the capabilities of human beings. I use my knowledge of computer programming and electronics to develop algorithms to control highly complex, humanoid robots. Many of the robots that

I work with have a human shape, so that eventually they can coexist in a space inhabited by humans without having to adapt to our surroundings. Our research focuses on three aspects. First, we aim to make robots as safe and reliable as possible so that they can assist humans as co-workers with difficult, dangerous and cumbersome tasks. Examples of areas of application include factory automation and construction, deep-sea oil and gas extraction as well as nuclear power plants. Second, we want to develop autonomous systems technology to make our lives easier and give us more time to enjoy with family and friends. Examples include self-driving cars and robot technology that can help around the house, such as autonomous vacuum cleaners and lawn mowers. Finally, I work with doctors and surgeons to develop prosthetics, a kind of robot that is used by patients who have had accidents and suffered injuries or lost limbs. By understanding how the human body works, we are able to restore some capability using robotic hardware. We develop artificial limbs for both the lower arm as well as legs. Our work also applies to situations where robots that can crawl or fly may be required to assist during a fire or in natural disasters like tsunamis or earthquakes to search for and rescue trapped people.

Q. What inspired you to take up the field of robotics?

Since my childhood, I was fascinated by machines or automatic mechanical devices. I have memories of playing with spring-wound mechanical toys, getting lost in the bazaars of Delhi, staring at printing machines and lathes at roadside factories as well as reading science fiction by authors such as Issac Asimov. It was this natural fascination for everything moving and the innate curiosity to understand what goes inside the box that provided me with the first inspiration towards robotics. After an undergraduate degree in computer engineering, I was curious to see how I could apply developments in the field of computers to make smarter robots. I was also fascinated by the human body itself—it is an incredibly versatile, multipurpose machine invented by nature. Since I was not a medical doctor or biologist, I thought the closest thing to understanding human motion capabilities was to create machines that can closely mimic them. This naturally led me to work in areas that were at the interface of machines and humans, leading to the prosthetics research.

Q. What is your typical day like?

Surprisingly, a research scientist like me does not have a typical day; every day brings exciting new challenges! Usually I start my day with a cup of coffee, and deal with urgent correspondence from my office in the informatics department. During term time, I teach a class of senior undergraduate and postgraduate students twice a week in the mornings on the subject of robotics and machine learning. I have regular lab meetings with my PhD students and postdoctoral researchers in my group and discuss weekly progress on research agendas and set new goals. I also have one-on-one meetings to discuss research topics on the whiteboard with my students in my office. A significant part of my day is spent implementing solutions on hardware. In between, I spend time writing up the results of our work in research papers as well as discussing ways to transform some of these ideas into novel products with commercial companies. I take a break for lunch in the afternoon, which is a fun affair where researchers from different fields informally chat about everything under the sun. I catch up with my secretaries on issues that I need to decide on in my role as institute director. I also chair institute faculty meetings to monitor research and progress of PhD students. In my role as a professor, I also have to travel extensively. This includes presenting papers at international conferences, attending project review meetings for our internationally funded projects as well as serving the community by being on peer review panels. Most of these trips are to really exciting cities in Europe like Lisbon, Barcelona, Paris, Zurich, etc., and there are some long-haul trips to the USA and Japan too. However, sadly, I am usually too busy to do any sightseeing! Sometimes I have to work weekends and late into the night to meet conference and project deadlines.

Q. What is the most important quality needed to be a successful robotics engineer?

One needs to possess an analytic thinking mind and develop strong fundamentals in science subjects such as mathematics and physics. Another very important quality is perseverance. Robotics involves creating conceptual solutions to real-world problems and then implementing them on real machines. The path from concepts and ideas to design, implementation on hardware (electronics, mechanics) and testing in the real world is filled with many steps and hurdles. It is easy to feel disappointed when a concept that seems to work perfectly on paper does not meet expectations due to mismatch in specifications and complex real-world conditions. Successful roboticists are able to overcome multiple setbacks on the road to success. Sometimes complex problems have relatively simple solutions. The quality to see through the clutter and complexity and discover simple breakthrough principles is another invaluable quality for a robotic engineer. Surprisingly, people with good design and artistic skills have a big role to play in robotics as well since it is not just about the mechanics. Good robots need to be compact, attractive and packaged appropriately to work in close contact with humans.

Q. Which is your favourite robot and what does it do?

My favourite robot is the humanoid robot Valkyrie, created by NASA. This robot was based on the Robonaut 2, which was designed to work in space. Valkyrie, on the other hand, is a robot built to work in environments that humans are used to on land. It has forty-four joints or degrees of freedom and is bipedal, meaning it walks on two legs unlike some robots that have wheels or chain tracks. Controlling such a complex but versatile robot is an exciting challenge that my group of researchers and I are

SCIENTIFIC PATHWAYS TO A BRIGHTER FUTURE

involved in. The robot was specifically designed for the DARPA Robotics Challenge (DRC) where robots were supposed to carry out a sequence of tasks such as walking over rubble or debris, opening doors, turning valves, climbing stairs, operating a power tool and getting into a 4X4 golf cart and navigating. The aim of the exercise was to develop robots that can autonomously (i.e., without human intervention) explore a natural disaster area like earthquake scenes or fire accidents and perform operations that a rescue worker would normally carry out. The larger object is to reduce the tasks humans have to carry out in dangerous and potentially life-threatening scenarios. The robot is nearly 1.65 metres tall, weighs around 150 kg and has many sensors like camera, laser-range scanner and touch sensors. It joints are moved by compact yet powerful electric motors and it has a large lithium-ion battery for power. It has several multicore computers on board to process the information and make decisions about what to do next and which motors to move appropriately. Although Valkyrie is a tremendously expensive robot (approximately $2.5 million dollars), I expect such robots to become very commonplace and much cheaper in ten to fifteen years due to the tremendous advances science is making.

 NOTE TO PARENTS

Robotics is one of the most innovative branches of science and technology. If your child wants to pursue a career in it, he or she can choose a career in industrial applications such as in automobile companies, consumer durables, machine-making organizations and even space-application organizations. Modern-day robots are constructed by highly professional organizations, and these are gradually developing in India also.

It is expected that in the not-so-distant future most regular factory work will be performed by robots who will be manned by workers. This would mean great opportunities for both robot designers and robot-maintenance scientists in such organizations. There are a large number of robotic engineers working in huge organizations such as Hindustan Aeronautical Limited, Bharat Heavy Electricals Limited, NASA, Boeing, Airbus, Ferrari, Siemens and other leading companies across the industry.

Another great opportunity for robotic engineering is in the field of academics and teaching. Leading universities in India and abroad are opening centres for robotic research, which are a point of convergence of multiple sciences.

If your kids are interested in robotics, it would be a good idea to provide them with access to books about programming and artificial intelligence. There are also a number of robotic kits and books aimed specifically at children which will give them a hands-on experience of basic robotics and help them make robots.

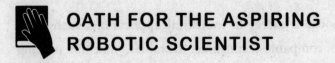

OATH FOR THE ASPIRING ROBOTIC SCIENTIST

'*I will be remembered for designing robots which helped humanity explore outer space and the deep sea or to solve the most pressing health-care challenges.*'

(Write this oath in the space below. You can also add new thoughts and goals for yourself as a robotic scientist.)

_____

_____

_____

_____

_____

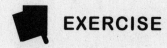 **EXERCISE**

Refer to the six different applications of robots in the future which we discussed earlier. Now, you have been asked by your company to design a new medical application robot. Identify the surgeries and actions which your robot will perform and draw a diagram of the robot here. Think of how many arms it will have, what features it will bear, and so on. It is important that the robot is able to turn and bend its arms, so ensure you make the right joints at the right places.

1   RoboCup-97: The First Robot World Cup Soccer Games and Conferences. http://aaaipress.org/ojs/index.php/aimagazine/article/viewFile/ 1391/1291,RoboCup-97

CHAPTER 2

'It is possible to fly without motors, but not without knowledge and skill.'

Wilbur Wright

Humankind has always been fascinated by flight. The Ramayana talks about a kind of aircraft called Vayuyan, which only the greatest and the mightiest kings owned. Greek mythology mentions Pegasus, a pure white horse with wings which belonged to the gods.

Do you know which was the first vehicle designed to make a man fly? It wasn't an aircraft, a rocket or even a hot-air balloon. It was a kite! In 1000 BCE, that is, about 3000 years ago, the Chinese invented giant kites which could carry a human being. These kites were flown over enemy armies to determine how big they were and which direction they were moving in. Of course, these kites weren't the safest fliers. Strong winds would turn them over or blow them off their target. Crashing was a problem too.

In 1010 CE, a monk named Oliver of Malmesbury became the first man to fly for some distance with the aid of wings. He jumped from Malmesbury Abbey, England, and flew a short distance before crashing to the ground and injuring himself. But this didn't stop others from continuing to design flights, keeping birds and even bats in mind. The problem of crashing, however, persisted. Many scientists were injured and some even lost their lives. The first man to land safely was Hezarfen Celebi who, in the seventeenth century, leapt from a tower in Galata (Turkey) and landed safe in a marketplace.

In 1804, roughly 200 years after the world's first safe landing, George Cayley built a glider. Parallel to this, humans started experimenting with hot-air and hydrogen balloons.

So far flights had had two major problems. First, they would crash. Second, they weren't exactly 'flights' in the true sense, because they never went upwards by themselves. They had to be taken to a height and thrown off, before they slowly descended. Though hot-air balloons went up on their own, there was no way to move them horizontally mid-air, and they would almost always get stuck there.

The challenge of flying a human being on a controlled and self-propelled flight frustrated numerous scientists—to the extent that in 1895 the revered scientist Lord Kelvin declared, 'Heavier-than-air-flying machines are impossible.' This declaration came as a blow to many flight enthusiasts of the time, though a few of them continued to try and invent newer ways to fly.

In 1892, two brothers from a very ordinary background set up a bicycle repair and sale shop in Dayton, USA. Both had been to high school but could not complete their diplomas because their family moved cities. This shop was called the Wright Cycle Exchange, and was owned by Wilbur Wright and his brother Orville Wright, who were to become the two legends of aviation history. It was here that the brothers started working on making a powered machine heavier than air which could fly—what we today call an aircraft. Between the years 1900 and 1902, they extensively researched the flight control system and experimented with different versions of unpowered gliders. The brothers correctly reasoned that a free-flying object had to be controlled along all three primary axes: roll, pitch and yaw. They built airplanes with moveable surfaces on the wing, elevator and rudder. Control of the surface shape was in the hands of the pilot. Even today, from the smallest to the largest of aircraft, all are controlled by these three motions and control systems.

The systems were complex, and with the propulsion system (engine) in place, the airplane looked too heavy to fly. But the brothers kept working on their models until they became the first people to fly a controllable, self-propelled, heavier-than-air machine on 17 December 1903. It was made of wood and muslin cloth. The biggest challenge was to design the engine. When the brothers looked for designs in various libraries they found nothing about air propellers, so they had to develop all the theory by themselves and then apply it to make a workable aircraft engine. The brothers tossed a coin to decide who would be the first one to fly. Orville won the toss. At 10.35 a.m., in Kill Devil Hills, where they had set up camp, Orville flew the first powered human flight for twelve seconds, covering 37 metres. (You can see a photograph of this in the image section.) The next two flights flown by Wilbur and Orville on the same day did slightly better, covering 50 metres and then about 60 metres. While these flights were only a little more than a long hop, they demonstrated that humans could fly machines heavier than air. It gave some much-needed confidence to the brothers as well as the scientific community. While resting on the ground after the flight, the aircraft got caught in a gust of strong wind and toppled over, suffering severe damage. It never flew again, and was given away to a museum. You can see it even today at the Smithsonian Aerospace Museum in Washington DC.

The brothers continued their journey and by 1905 they made their third design, Wright Flyer III. On one occasion, in October 1905, the plane flew over thirty-three minutes, covering a distance of about 40 km This was the 46th flight piloted by Orville. (Turn to the image section to see a photograph of this.) It not only proved the capability of a controlled flight but also the fact that flying in an aircraft was a lot faster than ground travel.

After the successful development of the first few airplanes, the Wright brothers continued to be involved in aerospace technology. Orville was one of the original members of the National Advisory Council on Aeronautics (NACA), which is the parent organization of the current NASA.

Their achievement marked the beginning of an era of human flight, leading to propellers, jet engines, fighter planes and huge commercial airliners in the following decades.

In 1914, the first commercial flight took place between St Petersburg and Tampa. It lasted twenty-three minutes and covered about 38 km. The pilot, Tony Jannus, maintained an altitude of merely 15 feet from the ground and had only a single passenger with him— Abram Pheil, who had paid roughly Rs 2.5 lakh (in today's value) for this short flight. Today, we can travel twice around the world for this amount, often at speeds just short of the speed of sound.

The Future of Aeronautics

Modern-day research is focused on four critical parameters in aircraft—cost, fuel efficiency, speed and safety. Two approaches are being followed worldwide to achieve these goals.

The first is the approach by traditional aircraft manufacturers— by using existing systems and engines and tweaking the final designs, cutting down some weight and adding better computers and autopilots to make the aircraft perform slightly better than the existing ones. By no means is this a futile effort, as significant positive results have come out of such efforts over time. For example, the *Boeing 787 Dreamliner*, which is now a part of the Air India fleet, has better composite material and a more efficient design than its competitors. Travelling at Mach 0.85 (85 per cent of the speed of sound), it consumes about 20 per cent less fuel than any other similar aircraft.

The second is the more radical approach where transformational aeronautics is being deployed to change existing designs, engines and standards completely. Two efforts particularly stand out in this domain. One is the NASA experimental plane series, popularly called X-planes. These are a series of aircraft designed to test experimental breakthrough technologies to push the barriers on flight. The first X-plane (called X-1) was flown way back in 1946, and was the first to break the 'sound barrier', that is, cross the speed of sound. The most famous X-series plane was the X-43A, also called Hyper X, which, using unique scramjet technology, flew at almost ten times the speed of sound, a record that remains unbroken still. However, these flights haven't been declared completely safe yet and are currently in the testing phase only. Many of them are unmanned and remotely controlled.

The other outstanding design to be ever conceived so far is that of the solar-powered aircraft called *Solar Impulse*. You can see a photograph of this in the image section. In 2010, the plane flew continuously for twenty-six hours. 'It has unlimited endurance,' explains André Borschberg, *Solar Impulse*'s co-founder. 'It can fly for weeks and months without stopping for fuel because it collects its energy from the Sun. The energy it collects during the daylight hours is enough to power it during hours of darkness as well.' *Solar Impulse II*, which will go around the planet in a single flight, is scheduled to be launched in 2015. So what is the trouble with solar flight right now? Well, even with the wingspan of a typical commercial plane and weighing a little more than a standard car, it can carry only a single person. Of course, with improvement in technology this is expected to improve manifold in the future, and we hope that by the year 2025 commercial airliners running on solar power will be a reality.

CONVERSATIONS WITH A SCIENCE TEACHER

Which is the largest aircraft in the world?

The *Antonov An-225 Mriya*, designed by the former USSR, is the largest aircraft in the world. It entered into service in 1988 and has maintained the record of being the largest aircraft for over twenty-six years now. It was originally designed to transport spacecraft; hence its large size. It has a takeoff weight of up to 640 tons, almost equivalent to ten battle tanks. It is 84 metres long.

The largest passenger aircraft is of course the Airbus A380, manufactured in 2005. It is designed to carry a maximum of 853 passengers on a single flight. It has a maximum takeoff weight of over 600 tons. The aircraft is a complex work of electronics, controls and safety standards. In fact, to operate all the control systems in the aircraft the total wiring inside each A380 extends to 530 km!

How high can an aircraft fly?

Modern aircraft can fly quite high into the second layer of atmosphere, which is called the stratosphere. Most jet engine aircraft fly at a height of 32,000 to 35,000 feet (approx. 9.75 to 10.66 km), which is about 3000 feet (approx. 914 metres) above Mount Everest, the highest peak in the world. They are the most fuel-efficient at this height. However, they can fly even higher if needed. The maximum height an aircraft can maintain over a sustained time is called 'ceiling'. Generally, the ceiling of fighter jets is much higher than that of passenger planes as they are lighter and also because they need a high ceiling to avoid missiles from the ground. For instance, the ceiling of the A380 is 43,000 feet (13.1 km) while the ceiling of an F-15 is over 65,000 feet (approx. 19.8 km). The ceiling of SU30MKI, the premier fighter of the Indian Air Force, is about 57,000 feet (approx. 17.37 km).

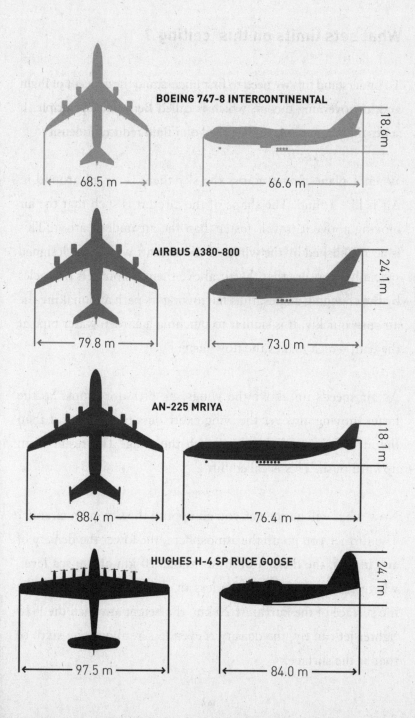

BOEING 747-8 INTERCONTINENTAL

18.6m

68.5 m

66.6 m

AIRBUS A380-800

24.1m

79.8 m

73.0 m

AN-225 MRIYA

18.1m

88.4 m

76.4 m

HUGHES H-4 SP RUCE GOOSE

24.1m

97.5 m

84.0 m

What sets limits on this 'ceiling'?

To understand this we need to first understand the concept of flight and its governing theory, which is called **Bernoulli's principle.** It states that an increase in the speed of a fluid reduces it density.

When a plane moves across the sky there is air all around it. Air is like a fluid. The shape of the aircraft is such that the air moving above it travels faster than the air underneath it. This is accomplished by the wings of the aircraft which are designed specially to ensure that the air above them encounters obstacles by the changing angles, thus narrowing its path and making the air rush quickly. It is similar to pinching a garden water pipe at the end, which makes the flow faster.

As air speeds up above the wings, its pressure drops. So the faster moving air over the wing exerts less pressure on it than the air moving slower underneath the wing. The result is an upward push. This is called 'lift'.

Now what will happen as you go up into the sky in an aircraft? The further you go up the atmosphere, the lower the density of air. In fact, the density of air at about 10 km above sea level, where commercial jets fly, is less than one-third its density at the surface of the Earth. At 20 km, the height at which the F-15 fighter jet can fly, the density is even lesser, about one-sixth of that at the surface.

Remember, pressure is proportional to density. Hence, with decreasing density, the upward pressure of the air passing below the surface of the wings also reduces. Hence, air can provide lesser and lesser lift to the aircraft, causing it to start falling. The maximum height to which air can support the aircraft is called ceiling. More powerful engines and lesser weight tend to increase the ceiling of the aircraft.

What fuel do aircraft use? Is it petrol or diesel?

Neither. Aircraft run on a special petroleum-based fuel called aviation fuel.

The most common aviation fuel is called jet fuel or aviation turbine fuel, which is used by aircraft powered by gas turbine engines. Most medium and large aircraft and military aircraft use jet fuel. It is usually colourless but can sometimes also be straw coloured. Avgas is another type of aviation fuel. This is used for aircraft which have internal combustion engines. Generally, only very small aircraft have internal combustion engines.

There are some special requirements for any aviation fuel. First, it should be pure and free from any particles that can choke the engine or its parts. Aircraft parts are sensitive and any impurities in the fuel can be very dangerous.

Second, the fuel should be capable of operating in very low temperatures. Commercial aircraft, when flying at a height of 25,000 to 30,000 feet, are operating at temperatures less than minus 30 degrees centigrade. Hence, it is important that aviation fuel does not freeze at such low temperatures. In fact, some special jet fuels, called Jet B fuel, do not freeze even at minus 60 degrees centigrade. This is used in very cold countries.

Third, the fuel has to provide the maximum energy possible to the aircraft engines. A high-energy fuel helps the aircraft carry lesser fuel, remain lighter and thus lift more passengers or cargo into the air. The technical term for this is 'calorific value', which refers to the amount of energy generated in joules for every kilogram of fuel burnt. Aviation fuels tend to have a very high calorific value.

What is the fuel efficiency of an aircraft?

Despite all the advancements, aircraft still consume a large amount of fuel, especially during the take-off and landing phases. At an average, domestic flights now cover 230 metres per litre of aircraft fuel, an increase of more than 40 per cent since 2000. There's also been progress for the heavier jets on international flights: the average is about 120 metres per litre of aircraft fuel. Fuel is indeed every expensive, and generally makes up about 40 per cent of the total cost of the airline companies.

So aircraft are burning tons of fuel high up in the atmosphere. Is that safe?

This is a very valid concern. In fact, the air transport industry is responsible for 2 per cent of man-made carbon dioxide emitted, which is about 700 million tonnes of CO_2 emissions every year. Since the year 1990, CO_2 emissions from international aviation have almost doubled.

Worse, the truth is that the pollution caused by aircraft emissions high up in the stratosphere is more hazardous to the environment and have a more harmful climate impact than that which is caused on the surface of the Earth by automobile emissions and other human activities. When an aircraft burns fuel, it produces carbon dioxide, vapour, nitrous oxides, sulphate and soot. In fact, experts estimate that aircraft emissions are responsible for killing more than 10,000 people annually due to breathing problems, lung cancer, heart diseases and climate change.

There is yet another problem. Have you seen a jet flying on a clear day? If you have, you would have also noticed a very long white smoky line streaming behind from its tail. This is called a contrail and it is a major climate hazard. It consists primarily of water droplets and ice, formed when water vapour released from burning jet fuel condenses at higher altitudes. Contrails may remain in the sky for many hours and can spread up to 2 km. What these contrails essentially do is trap the heat that would otherwise escape from the Earth, thus contributing to global warming. Studies have shown that night flights have stronger warming impact than daytime flights.

What can we do to address this challenge?

Reducing emissions from aircraft is a major concern, especially with the aircraft industry expanding so rapidly. One standard way has been to work on building better engines and working on better aircraft design which will reduce fuel consumption.

But scientists are also doing some transformational work. One of them is the development of the solar-powered aircraft that we discussed earlier in this chapter. Another approach is towards replacing traditional fuels with biofuels.

Biofuels are fuels that are extracted from crops such as corn and coconut, or special plants like jatropha or even algae. Globally there has been a significant effort in developing biofuels to make aircraft eco-friendly. It is estimated that the use of biofuels may reduce the emission effect of a regular aircraft by up to 85 per cent.

After extensive research, biofuels were approved for commercial use in July 2011. Since then, some airlines have experimented with biofuels on commercial flights. The first such test flight flew between London and Amsterdam and was operated by Virgin

Atlantic in February 2008. It used a coconut-based biofuel. In December 2008, Air New Zealand operated a jatropha-biofuel flight for over two hours. Then in June 2010, the Dutch military used waste cooking oil to run an Apache combat helicopter. In June 2011, the Dutch airline company KLM was the first to transport 171 passengers on an aircraft running on biofuel derived from cooking oil. This was followed by a series of regular flights running on biofuels. For instance, if you take a KLM flight from New York to Amsterdam you will probably be flying a *Boeing 777* aircraft running on recycled cooking oil!

These steps are expected to make aircraft not only fast and safe, but also green.

What is an autopilot? What functions can it perform?

Autopilots are devices which can control aircraft without constant human intervention. In the world of aeronautical engineers, the autopilot is more accurately described as the Automatic Flight Control System (AFCS). Typically an autopilot system is capable of controlling the engine for speed and height and the wings, elevator and rudder for direction. This is called a three-axis autopilot.

There are also one-axis autopilots which control only wings and help them level out, or two-axis autopilots which can control the wings and elevator.

Autopilots are controlled by a computer with several high-speed processors. There are multiple sensors located across the flight from which the main computer collects data about the flight. It reads data about weather, temperature and wind.

To activate the autopilot, the pilot inputs his desired functions; for example, the autopilot is asked to take the aircraft to a desired height or speed. The computer then reads the pilot's command and senses the aircraft's current status and weather conditions. It determines the path to take and starts working with the controls it has on the aircraft. The autopilot continues to read the data and adjust the controls until the desired input of the pilot is reached.

Okay . . . got it. So how often do pilots switch to this mode of flying?

Autopilots have immensely benefited pilots, who put the plane on autopilot almost regularly when on cruise mode. It frees them up for monitoring weather warnings and ensuring that the flight systems are operating well. It also helps them avoid fatigue and remain fresh and attentive for the landing process, which is the most difficult part of any flight.

Autopilots are also very useful for landing planes in difficult conditions, such as low visibility because of dense fog. This system is also called ILS or instrument-landing system. The most modern of such systems is called CAT IIIC, which allows completely automatic landing.

Why do planes shake during flights? Is this turbulence dangerous?

Basically, it is air pressure which keeps a plane flying up in the skies. Any minute disturbance in the air around the plane may cause it to shake. This is called turbulence. The moment pilots anticipate any alternations in the weather which may lead to turbulence they ask their passengers to fasten their seat belts in order to avoid any accidents.

The most common form of turbulence is called Clear Air Turbulence (CAT). Air in the upper skies almost moves like the rivers on Earth. It moves in snaking paths which are thousands of miles long but only a few miles deep and wide. The speed of such air currents can be up to 300 kilometres an hour. Now, depending on which direction the aircraft wants to fly in, it may choose to move into the air current or avoid it. It is similar to a ship which chooses to catch the favourable winds in the sails and furls them when it has to sail into the wind.

In the case of an aircraft, if a wind is opposite to the movement of the aircraft it is called a headwind, and if it is in the same direction it is called a tailwind. Pilots, like ancient sea captains, love tailwinds as it gives them extra speed; they avoid headwinds, which slow them down. Now, unlike a riverbank, pilots cannot see the edges of these air currents, or where they start and where they end. Sometimes, they may unknowingly move into or outside such major air currents, leading to a drop or rise in air pressure, consequently making the plane move up or down. Turbulence can also be caused by clouds and rains.

Turbulence can be of three types: light, moderate and severe. If you are on a one-hour flight, you are almost certain to experience a couple of instances of light turbulence which shift the plane by about 2 to 5 feet. Moderate turbulence happens only in about 1 per cent of the flight time, so you may experience this if you are a frequent flier. It causes aircraft to deviate by 10 to 20 feet and can be an uneasy time for passengers. Severe turbulence occurs so rarely that a pilot might experience it only once in his or her lifetime. It causes a plane to shift by a 100 feet and if passengers are not wearing seat belts it may cause injuries as well.

All types of turbulence are totally safe though it may cause discomfort to the passengers and make people nervous. Modern planes are designed to sustain even severe turbulence for several minutes. But remember to wear your seat belt when the pilot asks you to; it is for your own safety.

How can I become an aeronautical scientist?

Aeronautical science is one of the most exciting scientific expeditions of humanity. You can opt to be involved either with aircraft or with missiles and weapon systems if you choose this path. Aeronautic science covers everything from the design of planes to research on improving flight safety, fuel efficiency, speed and weight, or reducing system costs and using advanced technologies to meet customer needs. You can also choose to look after the maintenance of existing aircraft, whether fighter or commercial. Increasingly, aeronautical scientists are doing research on reducing the damaging impact of air travel on the environment.

All paths towards this career would begin with excelling in mathematics and physics. Within mathematics, learn advanced concepts in geometry and algebra. Geometry will help you determine and understand flight paths and read maps better, while algebra will help you solve complicated tasks like designing the correct angles and weights needed for aircraft and missiles. Aeronautics will also require you to read a lot of theory, so you should be good at languages also. The convergence of material science with aeronautics is imminent and hence knowledge of different lightweight materials and their properties is essential. You should also develop a keen attention to detail; not even minor flaws should go unchecked under your supervision.

You will have to opt for science with mathematics in your 10+2. India has some of the finest institutions in aeronautics, including most of the IITs and National Institutes of Technologies (NITs). I have seen many fascinating labs in Indian institutions, including the simulation lab at IIT Kanpur where students are constantly evolving newer models of aircraft, hovercraft and balloon-based flying objects. There are also some aircraft maintenance courses available at the bachelor's level in some private colleges. At the bachelor's and master's level of education the specializations you can choose include aerodynamics (study of interaction between air and flying bodies), aero-elastics (study of forces on aircraft), avionics (designing air controllers), propulsion (making aircraft engines) and composite materials (studying the materials used to make aircraft light and safe). In case you decide to pursue a master's level education in aeronautics, you will probably have to choose from one of these specializations for your major research and development assignment.

You can even choose to pursue some part of your aeronautics science training abroad. The top colleges known for aeronautics are mostly located in the United States, home of the Wright brothers. The Massachusetts Institute of Technology (MIT), Stanford University and University of Michigan are all well known for their aeronautics programmes. Outside USA, the University of Cambridge and National University of Singapore are also well known for this programme. In many institutions aeronautics is taught within the mechanical engineering department.

Planes are tall structures with very fine wiring and welding. Missiles are even more complex and minutely assembled. You will need to be strong and healthy to operate these systems. For this, you must ensure that you include proteins like milk and milk products in your diet and that you exercise. Avoid junk food! An unfit aeronautical engineer will find it difficult to make great aircraft. Learn some simple exercises from your parents or from the Internet which will protect your eyesight as well.

MEET THE EXPERT: DR A.P.J. ABDUL KALAM

The expert here is Dr A.P.J. Abdul Kalam himself, who has spent a large portion of his professional life in the field of aeronautics, especially in missile flight technologies. He's being interviewed by the co-author Srijan Pal Singh here.

Q. How did you get inspired to take up a career in flight?

Let me take you back to 1940–41, when India was still under the British, when Gandhiji walked in our villages and when the Second World War, the largest conflict in human history, was at its peak. I was in Class V. Because of the war, all resources were scarce, and the government rationed food and oil. This meant we could eat only what the government gave us, and if we wanted more, we had to go to the market and buy it at prices that were unaffordable for most. It was at this time that I took up my first job as a newspaper boy. My elder brother used to lend me his bicycle. It was slightly big for me and I would carefully balance myself on it, swinging right to left like a pendulum as it tottered across mud roads to reach the station at 5 a.m. in the morning. There I would pick up a bundle of Tamil newspapers and begin my task of delivering them to some local offices, some tea stalls and occasional homes. Unlike today, not every home got a newspaper; people would borrow the newspaper from their neighbours and share the news in conversations.

Before I set out on my brother's bicycle distributing the papers, I would spend time at the station itself. I used to sit on the bench there and open the bundle and carefully pluck out a copy of the daily newspaper *Dinamani*. The first page always caught my attention: it was usually filled with photographs of fighter aircraft and stories of the Second World War. Remember, this was during the London Blitz, the time when the conflict was over the skies of London. The German air force called Luftwaffe was sending hundreds of planes and bombers to attack the city and the British Royal Air Force had to deploy their full air force to defend their motherland. The stories would be about brave pilots from both the sides, and how they manoeuvred their aircraft and bombers. As a young boy, I used to love the stories of the pilots and their planes. I was curious about planes. I wanted to be a pilot myself.

Back in my village there were few people who could discuss aircraft. I was a disadvantaged child from a non-educated family; yet I had the advantage of being in the company of great teachers. My curiosity was fulfilled by a very special teacher when I was a ten-year-old boy in Class V. This was indeed a life-changing event.

My science teacher's name was Shri Sivasubramania Iyer. One day the topic of discussion in our class of sixty-five was 'how birds fly'. He went to the blackboard and drew a sketch of a bird with a tail, wings and head and explained how a bird flew. The same day he took us to the Rameswaram seashore where we saw dozens of seabirds flying. My teacher said, 'Look how the birds are flapping

their wings, now see how they change direction using their wings and tail. What is the locomotive force behind this flight—it is the life energy of the bird.' He told us that the same principles make an aircraft fly. Within an hour of our lesson, I learnt how birds fly.

What I learnt that day was unique. My teacher gave me an aim in life. Later I realized how important it was to study physics. I chose physics. I opted for aeronautical engineering, and then became a rocket engineer. Then a space technologist. That single lecture transformed my life and led me to make a profession out of my passion: rocket engineering and space flight.

Aeronautics, or the science of flight, is special to me. It was my first passion and my career began in this field.

Q. The next generation of flying is about supersonic and hypersonic speed. Which aircraft can achieve these velocities?

Sound travels at a speed of about 1200 kilometres an hour in dry air. This is referred to as Mach 1 speed. Anything that exceeds this speed is called supersonic sound. Speeds greater than five times the speed of sound (Mach 5) are often referred to as hypersonic.

The first supersonic flight was achieved in 1947 by an experimental aircraft, *Bell X-1*. Most modern fighter jets are capable of flying supersonic, at least for a limited amount of time. There have been some supersonic passenger jets as well, like the *Concorde* (which is now retired). Supersonic flights not only require massive engine power, they also generate tremendous heat as a result of air friction. A supersonic jet could easily have some of its parts heat up in excess of 300 degrees centigrade, which can damage the outer body of the aircraft. Hence, supersonic jets have special material such as titanium in some parts of their frame.

Missiles can also be made supersonic. BrahMos, a missile made by India and Russia, is the world's first supersonic cruise missile.

Hypersonic is the next higher domain of supersonic speed. It refers to speeds over 6000 kilometres an hour. Such speeds lead to extreme heating. While there is no manned fighter jet which reaches this speed, spacecraft carrying astronauts back into Earth from outer space are hypersonic. Such heating is very dangerous, and many spacecraft, including *Shuttle Colombia*, which was carrying astronaut Kalpana Chawla, meet severe accidents at these speeds.

 NOTE TO PARENTS

Air traffic has doubled every fifteen years in the recent past, and is expected to double again in the next fifteen years. By 2032, it is expected that there will 6.7 billion fliers annually across the world with about 33,000 commercial aircraft in operation, both figures almost doubling from the current numbers. The shift will be towards large, wide-bodied, fuel-efficient jumbo carriers. Moreover, since aircraft are generally replaced in fifteen to twenty years, there will be a significant demand for replacement of the existing fleets.

On the military side, the air force is the way forward for all major armed forces including India. The future will see air-based unmanned drones and missiles, with industries developing around these applications.

All forms of aeronautical applications will open new avenues for five major careers:

1. **Aeronautical engineer:** This career path involves research, design, development, maintenance and testing the performance of civil and military aircraft, including weapons and satellites. Such engineers are deployed by aircraft manufacturers such as Boeing, Airbus, Hindustan Aeronautics Ltd, India's Aeronautical Development Agency and NASA.

2. **Aeronautical researcher:** These scientists are the ones who break barriers and develop new technologies, materials and flight technologies which constantly transform the way aircraft fly. They are deployed by aircraft

manufacturers and also leading universities as part of their research in aeronautics.

3. **Aeronautical designer:** These are the people who work on the finer details of the aircraft, including designing and testing shapes and components. These experts are usually deployed by aircraft and aircraft component manufacturers.

4. **Aeronautical maintenance technician:** These are a set of highly-trained experts who ensure that aircraft are ready to fly the next morning; they also perform necessary repairs on them. They typically work with airline companies.

5. **Aeronautical consultant:** These are people who are experienced at providing business or technical solutions to airline operators, aircraft manufacturers, pilots or aviation policymakers. They may also be experts in airport management, fuel management and safety audits. They may be involved in testing and recording results for new experiments. Most aeronautical consultants must be registered with an accredited consultancy firm. Typically they work across all subsectors of aviation, including manufacturers, operators, military and academic institutions.

As you can see, aeronautics is a diverse career, with many possibilities and opportunities which will only increase in the future. We also expect significant progress in aircraft manufacturing within India, not just in the military but also commercial jets such as the soon to be launched seventy-seater commercial plane by HAL and NAL (National Aerospace Laboratories). Since Indian airline operators are also increasing in size and numbers, with the current fleet size of 400 expected to double in the next six years, the career of an aeronautic scientist is indeed a bright one.

In case your son or daughter aspires to pursue a career in aeronautics, you may like to give him or her books on the history and theory of aviation. There are some prominent aviation museums across India including the HAL Museum in Bangalore, the Indian Air Force Museum in Delhi and the Naval Aviation Museum in Goa which are storehouses of information and can ignite young minds. Many cities have clubs for aerodynamics enthusiasts who design their own model micro-aircraft. You may like to introduce your child to such a club. Many such interest groups are available online as well.

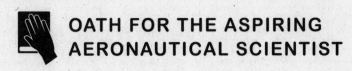

OATH FOR THE ASPIRING AERONAUTICAL SCIENTIST

'As a great aeronautical scientist, I will be remembered for developing new aircraft systems which will enable solar-powered flights with zero emission at supersonic speeds and ensure 100 per cent safety to passengers.'

(Write this oath in the space below. You can also add new thoughts and goals for yourself as a aeronautical scientist.)

_____

_____

_____

_____

_____

1 http://www.nasa.gov/audience/formedia/speeches/fg_kitty_
   hawk_12.17.03_prt.htm

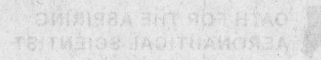

CHAPTER 3

PATHOLOGIST

On an average, a child born in the year 2014 can be expected to have a life expectancy of sixty-seven full years. Life expectancy means the average number of years a human being is expected to live.

Of course, this varies from country to country, but on an average the life expectancy in 2014 is about two-thirds of a century. Can you guess what the life expectancy of an average human being was in 1869, about 150 years ago, when Mahatma Gandhi was born? It was merely twenty-nine years!

And what about the time when Abraham Lincoln and Charles Darwin were born in circa 1800? A child born then had a life expectancy of only twenty-six years.

Go back further. Around 1 CE, when Jesus Christ walked the Earth, life expectancy was even lower—merely twenty-odd years. And of course, the caveman would expect to live even shorter—around fifteen years.

Why did this happen? Why did people live shorter lives about 150 years ago and what has made our lives almost three times longer than those born two millennia ago?

The answer is centred on one man, a French pathologist and the world's foremost expert on germs in his time—Louis Pasteur. He was born in 1822, and in his forties he made some remarkable discoveries about germs and their role in spreading illnesses. He invented some of the earliest methods to tackle them and make humans healthy again.

From the ancient times up to the 1850s, the most popular method of treating patients affected by acute problems, severe inflammation and various other diseases was a practice called 'bloodletting'. In simple terms, it meant making a cut on the patient's body and withdrawing blood from it. The belief was that the patient would be cured if the 'bad blood' was removed. Of course, the myth has been busted and bloodletting is now completely abandoned, but for centuries, most medical experts believed and practised this form of treatment. In fact, they developed special tools for ensuring smooth bloodletting, and in 1517 the surgeon Hans von Gersdorff wrote a famous book,

Field Book of Wound Medicine, where he illustrated with the help of elaborate diagrams specific parts of the body that were to be lacerated to induce bleeding for specific diseases. Obviously, this method never worked; in fact, many patients died not from the disease but from the blood loss that happened while the physician tried to cure the disease.

In the 1860s, however, Louis Pasteur discovered that airborne microbes were the cause of many diseases and that vaccinations were a way of preventing their spread. As you may have already learned, his initial work was not targeted at diseases, but at studying why food and beverages spoil over time. To understand why broth fermented over time, he placed the broth in flasks with filters to keep out the dust particles which would otherwise have entered them along with air. When he opened the flasks, he noticed the broth had not fermented, proving that fermentation happened from something outside the broth, which came in along with the dusty air. Thus Pasteur deduced there were germs in the air, which he believed were responsible for many of the biological changes that destroyed food and milk. These were called microorganisms and while humankind had not developed the capability to see these microorganisms fully then, Louis Pasteur and other pathologists proved their existence without even properly seeing them. Extending this idea, Pasteur wondered that if external air and particles could spoil food and milk, it was likely that external agents or germs could also be responsible for 'infecting' human bodies. He then proposed that in order to prevent diseases, these external, small, invisible microorganisms should be prevented from entering the human body through water, air or food.

During the latter part of the nineteenth century, this germ theory by Louis Pasteur became widely accepted. Better sewerage and water systems were introduced in many cities across the world, and hospitals were better sanitized. Around the same time, Joseph Lister, another famous pathologist and surgeon, developed antiseptics and showed how their use in operations could prevent the many infections associated with early surgery. Around the same time, German physicist Robert Koch made some key research in public health and microorganisms, including some groundbreaking work on tuberculosis, which won him the Nobel Prize.

This is how human life was extended by about three times—due to the study of germs and by controlling the diseases they cause. This is the science of pathology.

In one simple sentence, pathology means the study of disease and its causes. But pathology has often been defined as 'that branch of medicine which treats the essential nature of disease.'[1] The word 'pathology' comes from the Greek words 'pathos' meaning 'disease' and 'logos' meaning 'a treatise'. Similarly, all disease-causing organisms, such as different disease-specific bacteria, virus etc., are called pathogens. It is important to know that all microorganisms do not cause disease, and so it is not right to assume that every bacteria and virus is pathogenic.

Anatomical pathology is a common type of pathological science. It is the study of organs and tissues to determine the causes and effects of particular diseases. This branch of pathology involves the study and diagnosis of diseases based on the examination of surgically removed bodily specimens or sometimes of the whole body (autopsy). By studying these samples, such as blood, bone marrow or spit, anatomical pathologists can determine the pattern of disease and health of the overall organ and the body.

Another form of pathology is molecular pathology. This is a multidisciplinary field that focuses on disease at the submicroscopic level or even at the size of a single molecule. Aspects studied may include a mixture of anatomical pathology, clinical pathology, genetics, molecular biology and biochemistry. Molecular pathology is quickly becoming an integral component of medicine, providing important diagnostic, prognostic and therapy-related information as an adjunct to routine histopathology or the microscopic study of tissues in a variety of situations.

As explained, pathologists are doctors who study the cause and development of disease. Most choose a specialty such as genetics, diagnostics or forensic pathology.

Pathologists specialize in a wide range of diseases including cancer. Tissue samples are observed under a microscope and the cellular pattern observed to help determine if a sample is cancerous or non-cancerous (benign). Pathologists also employ genetic studies and gene markers in the assessment of various diseases.

The Future of Pathology

The world is full of microorganisms. There are typically 40 million bacterial cells in a gram of soil and a million bacterial cells in a millilitre of fresh water. There are approximately 5×10^{30} bacteria on the Earth (5 followed by 30 zeroes!) forming a mass which exceeds the weight of all plants and animals put together.

The unfortunate reality is that while we have understood most of the viruses, bacteria and other protozoa, there are many which are yet to be fully analysed. Moreover, as we develop medicines to fight one particular kind of microorganism, they too foster the ability to counter the effects of the medicine. This is called resistance to medicines. In this war-like situation, with germs on one side and medicines on the other, it is the task of the pathologist to continue to discover the new weaknesses of these germs which can be attacked by medicines.

Similarly, we are witnessing the rise of Gram-negative bacteria, which are resistant to antibiotics. These are bacteria that have a different outer layer compared to their counterpart, the Gram-positive bacteria. Unlike the Gram-positive bacteria, Gram-negative bacteria are difficult to detect and eliminate, so conventional antibiotics do not work on them. It is a challenge for future pathologists to study these Gram-negative bacteria and detect their weaknesses, which can be to the advantage of medical science.

There is yet another challenge for the pathologists. There are age-old common diseases that still affect humanity and consume many lives. Diseases such as diarrhoea lead to the death of more than a million children every year, half of them in India alone. Similarly, malaria, cholera, pneumonia, dengue and other commonly occurring infectious diseases are destroying a large number of lives, especially among the economically weaker sections of the society, for whom affording quality health care is a challenge. The new generation of pathologists needs to reinvent the old. They need to find effective, low-cost solutions to combat these age-old diseases and provide good health to every human being on the planet. We also need to find how to easily manufacture effective vaccines which can prevent people from contracting such diseases.

When Srijan and I were in Kentucky, USA, in 2011, at the University of Louisville, we met pathologists and doctors from the Brown Cancer Institute. They had found new weaknesses in particular cancer tissues and were in the process of developing a simple vaccine which could counter some forms of cancer at a cost lower than Rs 100. This is the future of pathologists—to work with other medical experts to counter diseases that plague humankind.

Another great challenge for the future pathologist lies in the emerging science of immunotherapy. In the treatment of some kinds of cancers, for instance, immunotherapy boosts the body's immune system instead of attacking the tumours directly. This and other types of immunotherapy are important scientific breakthroughs. Though the impact on the disease is not yet fully known, the results published so far have been positive. There is considerable research going on in the area of immunotherapy in the treatment of cancer and other diseases.

Another future evolution will be towards what is called the universal immunity vaccine. This means developing vaccines which when administered to a child will eradicate the chances of all types and variants of a disease from infecting him or her in adulthood. One such vaccine which is already in advanced stages of development is that of the universal vaccine against all kinds of flu. We are sure similar landmark vaccines will be developed against other diseases such as cancer, HIV, nervous diseases and infections such as diarrhoea. This is the job of future pathologists and it will require them to work closely with computer simulations and pharmacists (those who make medicines).

CONVERSATIONS WITH A SCIENCE TEACHER

I came across an article which mentioned that the name of the bacterium that causes tuberculosis is *Mycobacterium tuberculosis*. When I read more, I found all names of bacteria consist of two words. Why? What do these two words signify and what is the naming method like?

As soon as a new bacterium is discovered by scientists, it has to be given a new name, much like a newborn baby. The science of naming the new bacteria is called taxonomy and it follows certain strict guidelines. Bacteria follow the binomial nomenclature, a method developed by scientist Carl Linnaeus. The name of any bacterium consists of two names: the genus followed by the species.

Before a bacterium is given a name, it needs to be classified either by its shape, clustering pattern, food source or mobility. This is called the genus.

The rules of naming usually use Latin or Greek words. The genus has the first letter written in capital while the species is written in small letters completely. The species are named according to their occurrence, country of origin, name of the discoverer and other such related factors.

Let us take a few examples.

Escherichia coli: Here the genus is *Escherichia*, named after its shape, a straight rod, while *coli* stands for where it occurs (colon in the stomach of animals).

Vibrio cholera: Genus is *Vibrio*, named after the shape (comma shaped), while the species, *cholera*, is named after the fact that it causes cholera in humans.

What are the different types of bacteria and how small are they?

The size of bacteria varies according to their type and function and also where they live. The bacteria in our body may be different from the bacteria present in other mediums, whether air or water. Broadly, bacteria can be classified into three categories according to their shape: the spherical bacteria known as coccus, the rod-shaped bacteria known as bacillus, and the twisted-shaped bacteria known as spiral.

The spherical or coccus bacteria may be oval, elongated or flattened on one side. But they will be somewhat round in shape. The diameter of a coccus will vary from 0.5 to 1.0 micrometres, which is approximately one-thousandth part of a millimetre. The bacteria *Neisseria meningitidis*, which causes the disease meningitis, is an example of such bacteria.

Rod-shaped or bacillus bacteria, which are slightly larger, measure from 0.5 to 1.0 micrometres in breadth and 1.0 to 4.0 micrometres in length. *Lactobacillus bulgaricus*, which is used to produce yogurt and cheese from milk, is an example of rod-shaped bacteria.

The third type, spiral bacteria, is the largest in size, and can measure from 1.0 to 100.0 micrometres in length. These bacteria look like capsules. Besides these three major shapes, there are other shapes too, such as comma shaped (called Vibrio) and other smaller groups.

The smallest bacteria found in the human body, which cause influenza, are 0.2 to 0.3 micrometres broad and 0.5 to 2.0 micrometres long. However, the largest bacteria, called *Thiomargarita namibiensis*, found in Africa, can grow up to three-fourths of a millimetre and is visible to the human eye. Of course you still have to focus really hard to see it!

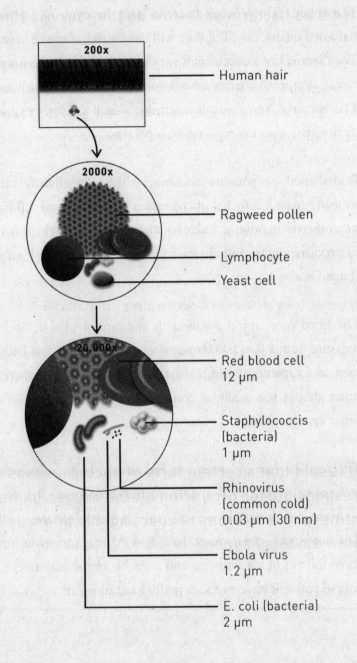

200x

Human hair

2000x

Ragweed pollen

Lymphocyte

Yeast cell

20,000x

Red blood cell
12 μm

Staphylococcis
(bacteria)
1 μm

Rhinovirus
(common cold)
0.03 μm (30 nm)

Ebola virus
1.2 μm

E. coli (bacteria)
2 μm

What do bacteria eat? How do they survive?

Different types of bacteria use different sources of energy to survive. The most basic form is where bacteria, like plants, use light from the Sun to generate energy for growth. These are called phototrophic bacteria. Some of these draw carbon from atmospheric carbon dioxide.

Other bacteria can generate their energy from inorganic compounds like nitrogen and sulphur and are called lithotrophic bacteria. Some of these bacteria might even be anaerobic, which means they do not need oxygen to live and hence are not dependent on atmospheric air for their survival.

There is yet another type called organotrophic bacteria; they derive energy from organic compounds (those with carbon). They too can be aerobic (requiring oxygen) or anaerobic.

It is said that a certain form of bacterium was responsible for producing all the oxygen in the atmosphere millions of years ago. Is this true? How did this happen?

Yes, many scientists believe that the abundant appearance of oxygen was a result of the biological activities of bacteria, mostly of the autotrophic type. This process is called the Great Oxygenation

Event (GOE) and it happened about 2.3 billion years ago. The bacteria responsible for this process are called cyanobacteria, and they appeared about 200 million years before the Great Oxygenation Event. Before this, all free oxygen produced was chemically captured by dissolved iron or other organic matter, called oxygen sinks. But cyanobacteria, which were expanding in number, kept pumping more and more oxygen, till these sinks of oxygen became completely saturated and could not absorb any more oxygen. This excess oxygen entered the atmosphere.

Remember, till then the Earth did not have animals or organisms like us which needed oxygen. The presence of oxygen in the atmospheric air led to the appearance of a new kind of organism, which thrived on other organisms, and which eventually evolved into more complex life forms such as birds, animals, fishes and humans.

What about viruses? How small are they? Are they alive?

Viruses are so small that some of them can even enter a bacterium and infect it. In fact, viruses are typically 1000 times smaller than a bacterium. They are between 17 to 300 nanometres long, one nanometre being one-billionth of a millimetre. As you may have guessed, they cannot be seen with an ordinary microscope; you will need a special electron microscope to view a virus.

Unlike human cells, plant cells or bacteria, viruses don't contain enzymes which are needed to carry out chemical reactions that support life. Instead, viruses carry only one or a couple of enzymes that decode their genetic instructions, or simply carry the 'identity card' of the virus. So, a virus must have a host cell (bacteria, plant or animal) in which to live and make more viruses. Outside a host cell, a virus cannot function and behaves like a non-living thing. For this reason, viruses tread the fine line that separates living things from non-living things.

What exactly is cancer? Which germ causes it?

Cancer is amongst the oldest diseases to plague humanity.

Cancer is simply a disorder of the cells where bad cells multiply and grow into tumours and affect all other body organs. Our entire body keeps regenerating new cells as the old ones keep dying. This varies from organ to organ. For instance, your taste buds are destroyed and replaced completely every ten days![2] The lungs are regenerated every two weeks. Even our entire skin gets replaced every four weeks and bones are refreshed in every ten years. However, the brain and eye cells are rarely replaced in full.[3]

Now, every time a cell is regenerated there is a very small chance that the new cells are 'bad' and not an exact copy of the replaced cell. Let us understand how this can happen.

The process of creating new cells and even the behaviour of existing cells is governed by our 'genes'. Cells control most of their functions by producing specific 'proteins' that act almost like on and off switches for a cell. But it is the genes which act as codes or instructions and tell the cells what proteins to produce.

Cells make multiple types of proteins and there is a single type of gene for each type of protein. Since one cell can have many different genes, it can prepare all those types of proteins too.

Now suppose a gene, or an instruction set, is damaged, so the cell cannot read it properly. It cannot control the manufacturing of protein—the on and off switch is now damaged. Sometimes, it may keep on producing excessive protein, and at other times it may not produce any protein at all. This is called mutation.

Now, let us come to the problem of cancer. There are three specific types of genes that are relevant to this:

1. Oncogenes or genes that encourage the cell to multiply
2. Tumour-supressor genes or genes that stop the cell from multiplying[4]
3. DNA-repair genes or genes that repair other damaged genes

Oncogenes are usually needed especially when there is a wound. These quickly tell the cells to start multiplying. Now suppose oncogenes are damaged and they tell the cells to keep multiplying without stopping—this would lead to an uncontrolled growth in cells, a condition of cancer.

Similarly, if the tumour-supressor genes are damaged, that cell will never turn off its multiplication, and will keep getting replaced and continue growing. Another case of potential cancer.

The DNA-repair genes are unique as they are responsible for detecting and repairing any faults in the genes. They are supposed to fix errors in the genes and stop wrong cells from replication. If these genes are damaged, all the errors will be unchecked and impossible to rectify.

Even with errors in genes the body has a defence mechanism, and that is why every mutation cannot turn into cancer. About half a dozen different mutations must occur before this happens. Cells often destroy themselves if they have a mutation. Even if they don't, the immune system might recognize them as abnormal and kill them. This means most precancerous cells die before they can cause cancer. Only a small number become cancerous.

Cancer is hence not induced by any bacteria or virus. It is caused by genetic flaws, which are hereditary (passed from parents to their children). Moreover, there are carcinogenic (cancer causing) substances like nicotine which make cells and genes more susceptible to damages and errors, and hence rapidly increase the risk of cancer. That is why smoking tobacco and other such bad habits should be avoided.

There are more than a hundred different types of cancer. Most cancers are named after the organ or type of cell in which they originate. For example, cancer that begins in the colon is called colon cancer.

I have heard a lot about how HIV is a virus which medicines are unable to treat. Can you explain why?

Viruses such as the Human Immuno-deficiency Virus (HIV) exhibit uncommon characteristics of mutating (changing their nature) with the ability to generate variants within the infected person—sometimes many variants within a single day. HIV has also developed the ability to attack the very cells in humans which are supposed to fight off the infections (called CD4 lymphocyte, a type of white blood cell) and they can remain hidden within the cell for months and years. Our current drugs cannot attack viruses hidden within cells; hence they are unable to cure HIV. There is a depiction of this virus in the image section.

So how can a pathologist defeat such clever viruses?

We need to find ways to enable medicines to identify such viruses. They must certainly leave some trace and clues when they hide in the cells, which pathologists need to find, much like detectives. But yes, the task is challenging.

There have been significant efforts in this domain. For instance, at the University of California, San Diego (USA), scientists ran molecular simulations to capture the movements of a small pocket of protein on the virus's surface that they believed could be targeted by drugs. This could prevent the replication of the virus. Using the pocket as a target, they used computer simulations to screen thousands of compounds and tested sixteen of them for their ability to block HIV infection in human tissue cultures. Ultimately, they discovered two complex compounds that inhibit HIV replication and effectively block the activity of replication of the virus (a process called Reverse transcriptase). Thus, computer scientists and pathologists worked together to find the weaknesses of this difficult virus.

In late 2007, a group of German researchers used a bone marrow transplant to treat a person who was affected by cancer and AIDS virus (HIV). The patient was transplanted with bone marrow from a donor who had a genetic mutation known to give a natural immunity to the HIV for three years. When he was tested again in 2010, the virus was completely eliminated and was not found hiding anywhere.[5] Similarly, in 2014, University of New South Wales in Sydney declared that two patients, both Australian men, apparently became HIV-free after receiving stem cells to treat cancer.[6]

Of course, this type of surgical transplant or complex treatment is a difficult process and ideally we should have vaccines or medicines against these diseases. But it would be a challenging study for future pathologists to find what gives special immunity to some people against these clever viruses.

How are vaccines developed?

A vaccine is a preparation that improves the immunity of the human body against a particular set of diseases. Most vaccines are made from agents which resemble the disease-causing microorganism. These may be weakened or even dead microorganisms of the disease. These are administered to the human body, usually to younger children, through either injections or orally. These are called antigens.

The immunity system of the body identifies these antigens. Since these antigens are weak, they are unable to affect the body adversely. In the meantime, the immune system starts building proteins that can counter these antigens. These are called antibodies. Antibodies are produced by white blood cells called lymphocytes, also known as B cells. The main purpose of the B cells is to create antibodies to fight infection. Soon the weak antigens are killed, but the body learns about the new infection and stores the antibodies for the rest of the person's life. Next time, when the stronger, actual bacteria or virus attacks, the body is already prepared to fight them off with the antibodies. In fact, this is how you should study. If you have even briefly glanced through your lesson before going to class, when the actual class begins you will be able to understand much better and it will also help you in the exams!

That is interesting. I wonder who designed vaccines . . .

It all happened because of the power of observation and scientific scrutiny. In 1796, an English physician named Edward Jenner decided to prove a theory that had been circulating for some time. You see, in those times, smallpox used to kill millions of people worldwide. Closely resembling smallpox was another disease named cowpox, but it was a less serious disease, which milkmaids often caught through exposure to infected cows.

Jenner noticed that the milkmaids who had contracted cowpox were later immune to smallpox. Jenner tested this theory when he took some infected cowpox matter and exposed an otherwise healthy boy, named James Phipps, through a cut in his arm. After the boy had caught and recovered from cowpox, Jenner exposed him to smallpox through an injection. The boy remained healthy, and thus the world's first vaccine was created. Jenner submitted a paper to the Royal Society in 1797 describing this experiment, but was told that his ideas were too revolutionary and that he needed to submit more proof. Undaunted, Jenner experimented on several other children, including his own eleven-month-old son. Finally, in 1798, the results were published and vaccines were born. Jenner was widely criticized and ridiculed with cartoons depicting people turning into cows after vaccination. (You can see a cartoon from 1802 mocking Jenner in the image section.) But, like a true scientist, Jenner believed in his success and kept working on more and more vaccines. Interestingly, the cows, for their part, were honoured when the term 'vaccine' was coined, 'vacca' being Latin for cow.

How are vaccines different from antibiotics?

An antibiotic is an agent that either kills or inhibits the growth of a microorganism inside the body. Unlike vaccines, which help to build up the immune system against microorganisms, antibiotics directly attack the microorganism and stop their growth.

Humans have unknowingly been using various antibiotics from different plant and animal products to treat diseases for over two millennia. In 1877, Louis Pasteur and Robert Koch observed that an airborne bacillus could inhibit the growth of *Bacillus anthracis*. They called this phenomenon antibiosis (or against the life of bacteria). This was later renamed antibiotic. The first effective antibiotic came about fifty years later, in 1928, when Alexander Fleming, a Scottish scientist, discovered penicillin. He was awarded the Nobel Prize for this discovery. Quite by accident Fleming noticed that a number of disease-causing bacteria in his discarded Petri dishes had been killed by a fungus of the genus *Penicillium*. Fleming postulated that the effect is mediated by an antibacterial compound he named penicillin.

Of course, today we have a number of antibiotics. The World Health Organization estimates that antibiotic treatments add an average of twenty years to all of our lives.

The problem is that even bacteria and virus are learning to be resistant to old antibiotics and hence new variants have to be invented continuously to counter their power of resistance building.

I have heard that antibiotics are made from many different sources. Which are these?

Antibiotics can be sourced from multiple natural and synthetic agents. This is very important as the effectiveness of an antibiotic against a particular disease depends on the source from which it is taken. For example, a frog's skin contains more than 100 potentially bacteria-killing substances which can eventually evolve as drugs. Ants are the source of some antifungal drugs.

Here is a list of the some of the strangest sources of medicine and antibiotics:

SOURCE OF ANTIBIOTIC	USED TO CURE
Cockroach brain	bacterial meningitis
Catfish's skin mucous	lung infection caused by the bacterium *Klebsiella pneumoniae*
Alligator's blood	diabetic ulcers and severe burns
Ocean sediments	anthrax
Chemical compound from recycling old LCD TVs	bacterial meningitis, boils

How can I become a great pathologist?

Pathology is a very diverse and expansive stream of science, as there are thousands of bacteria, viruses and other microorganisms to study and experiment on. Pathologists need to be precise, knowledgeable in science and have the ability to work under pressure.

The best path towards becoming a great pathologist begins with a standard MBBS, the bachelor's degree needed to become a doctor. This has to be done after the 10+2 level, through various highly competitive national-level examinations. To successfully clear these exams, you must do well in physics, chemistry and biology. Pathologists are especially interested in the convergence of chemistry, which makes the drugs, and biology, which studies the characteristics of microorganisms. Hence, it is important that you read as much as you can, and have a thorough knowledge of these two subjects.

The MBBS course, spanning four to five years, covers a number of subjects which lead into pathology—including anatomy, forensic medicine, clinical medicine and chemical pathology, haematology (the study of blood), immuno-pathology and microbiology.

After your MBBS, you can opt for a master's degree in pathology or microbiology from any well-known Indian or international university. Almost all major medical institutions offer these courses. Besides the MBBS course, one can also opt for a B.Tech course in microbiology, though the focus in these courses is more on industrial applications.

To be a successful pathologist, you should be interested in the technical aspects of medicine and treatment and a major part of your work will involve using the microscope. Hence, it is also important to ensure that your posture and eyes are taken good care of. For this, I recommend you consume healthy food, with lots of vitamin A and other nutrients. You should also maintain a good regime of physical exercise to stay fit. Additionally, to keep yourself updated, you could subscribe to some of the well-known science journals, or read them in a library. Find out the latest articles about new forms of diseases and their cures, especially about genomics, stem cells and targeted medicine. Make a small science notebook, or a document on your computer, where you can record all these findings.

The India Association of Pathologists and Microbiologists, the Indian Association of Oral & Maxillofacial Pathologists and the Molecular Pathology Association of India are some of the prominent pathological organizations in the nation.

 ## MEET THE EXPERT: DR ASHOK VIKHE PATIL

President – International Association of Rural Health and Medicine
Executive Chairman – Pravara Rural Education Society

Q. Please tell us about the kind of work you do in the field of medical sciences and research.

I have been working in the area of education and rural health since 1986. I have worked with various NGOs, including some international NGOs as well as UN organizations.

The main objective of the rural health programme is to provide accessible and affordable health care to the rural people. The biggest problem faced by the rural population is access to health care due to the lack of resources, manpower and infrastructure. I took over the Pravara Medical Trust and developed many initiatives, some of which are -

i.   Reduction of Fertility, Morbidity and Mortality in selected 100 villages of Ahmednagar district, funded by USAID in 1992

ii. Health camps taking health care to the doorsteps of the people.

iii. eHealth and telemedicine

iv. Herbal Drugs for Arthritis

v.   Probiotic Patents – Diarrhoea is the single largest cause of death among children in India. I have patented a probiotic based on *Lactobacillus reuteri* which can kill the pathogenic bacteria, virus and protozoa.

vi. Research on salt-tolerant genes and stress-tolerant genes – The productivity of Indian farming is dependent on the weather. We either have drought or we have too much rain, which causes salinity in the soil. I worked with some international universities which identified the genes in dicotyledons which were stress tolerant and some genes which were salt tolerant.

vii. Paediatric cardiac surgeries

viii. We developed a workshop to produce calipers for physically challenged children. The path was shown to us by Dr Kalam using the FRO which he found during his satellite work.

ix. Developing a model for Sustainable Health & Development in 235 villages, funded by Swedish International Development Agency

x.   The Healthy Village movement was pioneered to build a sustainable healthy village.

xi. Village food bank – This idea was mooted to help villagers and pregnant women overcome food problems in times of scarcity,

xii. I developed Pravara Rural Medical College into the world's first rural medical university in 2005, under the name of Pravara Institute of Medical Sciences.

xiii. I am the President of the International Association of Rural Health and Medicine, working on policies and systems around the world

xiv. Authored the Loni Declaration at the National Conference on Rural Health, Loni, which became the basis of the National Rural Health Mission

Q. What inspired you to take up a career in this field? What motivated you to take up the cause of rural health care?

Being born and brought up in a remote village as a child, I experienced and witnessed the miseries of the rural poor. They were deprived of education and health care which resulted in high morbidity and mortality.

My grandfather, Late Padmashree Vitthalrao Vikhe Patil, a pioneer of the cooperative movement in India, changed the scenario by starting the first cooperative sugar factory in Asia in 1948. He convinced the small and poor farmers to join him in starting a cooperative sugar factory so that they could get remunerative prices for their sugar cane. This enabled them to break out of the vicious cycle of poverty.

He realized that education was the key to sustainable development in society. He believed in gender-sensitive education, where rural girls would be given equal opportunities to avail education. After starting the Pravara Rural Education Society in 1964, he realized that the provision of health care was an equally important aspect of improving quality of life. Thus the Pravara Medical Trust was founded in 1975 with this aim in mind.

My village didn't have electricity, drinking water or any other infrastructure such as roads, sanitation etc. My school had mud flooring and we had to collect cow dung every Wednesday to make a slurry with which we made a floor for us to sit on. Nobody in my school, including me, had any sort of footwear. We studied by the light of a kerosene lamp, which had an open flame. That's how I was inspired to carry on the noble work.

The rural health care is the most neglected sector of our economy. The villages do not have competent manpower, infrastructure or the financial resources to attend to their health issues. Realizing this, I returned from Sweden in 1986 to take on this challenge.

Q. So many new forms of diseases are coming up every year. We saw bird flu, swine flu and then Ebola. How do you think we can address these new diseases with new medicines?

The world is now a global village and with the dynamic global economy, the diseases are crossing the geographical boundaries. The diseases are caused by new agents and new vectors. The mode of transmission of diseases has changed.

Many existing drugs are no longer effective for treatment of the diseases for which they were discovered. For example, the drugs/ antibiotics for malaria, tuberculosis and typhoid are not showing any effects anymore and now we have the problem of Total Resistant Antibiotics.

We not only have to face the problem of new diseases but we also have to deal with the old ones because there has been indiscriminate and irrational use of drugs/antibiotics in India. This has caused drug-resistant organisms due to mutations and we will have to face this huge challenge in the coming decade. The drug and other chemical industries are causing water pollution, adding a bigger dimension to the issue.

Penicillin is still used as the first choice of antibiotic in Sweden but we, in India, have started using the fifth generation of the antibiotic to overcome infections.

We should pay more attention to the preventive aspects in health care so that the chances of transmission are reduced. While controlling a typhoid epidemic in a nearby town, I found that the entire infected population was resistant to the first choice of drug and we had to proceed with an expensive higher antibiotic.

Having studied the problem of bird flu with the WHO, I found that the disease was a product of unhygienic conditions in animal care and culling.

In case of dengue fever, we have totally failed in curtailing mosquito breeding.

We should concentrate on identifying the agent, vector and transmission since the disease is the result of a process. We then can eradicate the disease. We have to cut across cultural, religious, social traditions and beliefs and address the issue in a logical and scientific manner.

Q. What is your message for those aspiring to take up a career in either studying diseases or finding new cures and medicines for diseases that affect humankind?

There are about 7000 diseases while we have found cures for only 500.

We have been treating diseases with the same kind of treatment for all types of patients. There is a need to study evidence-based medicine. The traditional approach of applying a therapy to a broad group of patients is no longer the best path forward, particularly for those diseases for which we do not have a treatment or cure. We need to use technological tools such as genetic screening to target the right treatments to the right racial or ethnic groups.

The DALY (Disability Adjusted Life Years) is a tool to quantify the Burden of Disease from Mortality and Morbidity. The disease pattern is changing and now the leading causes of DALY are going to be cardiovascular diseases, respiratory infections, stroke, cancer, psychological (mental and behavioural disorders) and trauma (accidents). The medical sciences need to work on the preventive, curative and rehabilitative aspects of these diseases.

The Ayurvedic system of medicine needs to conduct more clinical research since many pharmaceutical companies are already using herbal plant molecules to develop better drugs. Since arthritis is one of the causes of rural poverty, I developed a drug from a plant for its treatment. Modern medicine hasn't succeeded in curing this disease and is only treating the symptoms which are beyond the reach of the poor.

Today about 90 percent of the research is directed towards 10 percent of the diseases. This is done with an ulterior motive of profiting and is catering to the needs of the rich. Only 10 percent of the USD 55 billion global expenditure on health research is devoted to diseases or conditions that account for 90 percent of the global burden of disease. Of the 1200 drugs developed between 1971 and 1996 only 3 were antimalarials. The youth of today should research cost-effective remedies that address the needs of the poor..

Another area that the youth of today should concentrate on is bio medicine. Bio medicine is a branch of medical science that applies biological and other natural science principles to clinical practice. Bio medicine involves the study of physiological processes with methods from biology, chemistry and physics.

 NOTE TO PARENTS

Medicine is going to be one of the biggest areas of scientific growth in the future—as our foremost quest will be to make human beings healthy and ensure everyone a long life. Pathology will be a major factor in understanding diseases, studying the pathogens which cause them and identifying the best solutions to counter them.

Pathogens are evolving too and becoming immune to medicines, and all the while new kinds of bacteria and viruses are also forming. Hence, the role of pathologists in the near future will be significant.

In the times ahead new concepts in medicine, such as genomics, will become prominent, which will customize health care and medicine for every individual based on their health profile. Pathologists will be needed to provide customized analyses for every individual—so we will probably see a convergence of pathology, medicine and information technology. Young pathology aspirants must therefore develop an interest in all these three aspects.

Pathologists are now working as part of large-scale organizations, multinational pharmaceutical companies, international health-care organizations and government health-care facilities, as an integral part of the health care system. Pathologists can also become entrepreneurs and set up their own private practices.

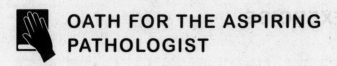

OATH FOR THE ASPIRING PATHOLOGIST

'As a great pathologist, I will be remembered for developing a new understanding of microorganisms which will improve human health and find cost-effective ways to detect and solve the problems of malaria, diarrhoea, cholera and HIV. Also, I will never induce diagnostic pain to my patients by recommending them tests which they do not need.'

(Write this oath in the space below. You can also add new thoughts and goals for yourself.)

_____

_____

_____

_____

_____

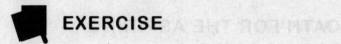

EXERCISE

Let us try to recreate the experiment done by Louis Pasteur which became the basis for germ theory. Just like Louis Pasteur you will need some milk, three vessels, some transparent covering material and a watch or clock for this experiment.

Take about half a litre of fresh, unboiled milk. Now divide this into three equal portions. Ask your mother or any adult to boil one of these portions and then cool it down to room temperature. Put this in one out of the three identical bowls. You now have three samples, two are unboiled (Samples A and B) and the third one is boiled (Sample C).

Cover one of the bowls containing unboiled milk with a tight transparent cover (Sample B).

Now it is time to start our experiment. Leave Sample A out in the open where it is exposed to open air, say in your balcony. Place sample B next to it. Then place sample C in the refrigerator (or some other well-covered cool place). Let an hour pass by. Then observe the samples after every thirty minutes to see whether the milk has spoiled in them. Fill in the following table after five hours.

MATERIALS:

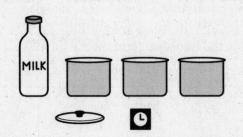

STEP 1:

A   B   C

STEP 2:

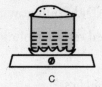

C

STEP 3:

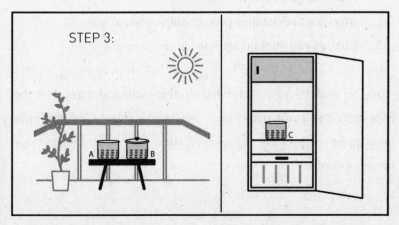

TIME	WHETHER THE MILK IN SAMPLE A HAS SPOILED	WHETHER THE MILK IN SAMPLE B HAS SPOILED	WHETHER THE MILK IN SAMPLE C HAS SPOILED
1 hour			
1.5 hour			
2 hours			
2.5 hours			
3 hours			
3.5 hours			
4 hours			
4.5 hours			
5 hours			

Answer the following questions carefully. Remember to think well before you answer. Did you know that back in the 1860s these sample questions led to the evolution of germ theory?

1. Which sample spoiled first?
2. Which sample spoiled last, or didn't spoil at all?
3. What do you thinking boiling did to the milk?

Also, to add to your knowledge, the technical term for the experiment you just performed is pasteurization. Can you now investigate the process of pasteurization further and write your findings here?

_____

_____

_____

_____

_____

To what temperature is milk heated in the pasteurization process and to what temperature is it cooled and how fast?

_____

_____

_____

_____

_____

1   Definition of Pathology. http://www.medicinenet.com/script/main/art. asp?articlekey=6387

2   How Do Our Taste Buds Change As We Age? http://www.growingraw.
    com/loss-of-taste-and-smell.html
3   'Believe it or Not, Your Lungs Are Six Weeks Old and Your Taste Buds
    Just Ten Days! So How Old Is the Rest of Your Body?', *Daily Mail UK*.
    http://www.dailymail.co.uk/health/article-1219995/Believe-lungs-weeks-
    old--taste-buds-just-days-So-old-rest-body.html
4   Tumor Suppressor Genes. http://users.rcn.com/jkimball.ma.ultranet/
    BiologyPages/T/TumorSuppressorGenes.html
5   Maggie Fox, German Doctors Declare 'Cure' in HIV Patient.
    http://www.reuters.com/article/2010/12/15/ us-aids-transplant-
    idUSTRE6BE68220101215
6   'Cancer Treatment Clears Two Australian Patients Of HIV', *Nature
    Magazine*, December 2014

CHAPTER 4

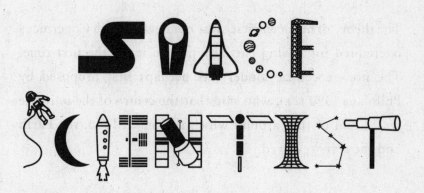

The battle for heliocentricity

'There is talk of a new astrologer who wants to prove that the Earth moves and goes around instead of the sky, the Sun, the Moon . . . the fool wants to turn the whole art of astronomy upside down,' said the much revered Martin Luther, one of the pioneers of the Protestant Reformation. He was reacting to the equally famous sixteenth-century astronomer Nicolas Copernicus and his remarkable theory that it was the Earth which went around the Sun and not the other way round. This theory came to be known as heliocentricity.

Copernicus was the first astronomer to mathematically disprove the age-old geocentric belief—that the Earth was the centre of the universe and that everything—the Sun, Moon, stars—went around it. Unfortunately, Copernicus suffered the same fate as many other astronomers before him—his theory ran into a collision course with the views of the Church.

The theory of heliocentricity was not new, though Copernicus is credited for having partially proven it for the first time. The non-geocentric model was perhaps first proposed by Philolaus (390 BCE), who said that the centre of the universe was a ball of fire, around which the Sun, Moon, the Earth and the stars revolved.

A century later, in 270 BCE, Aristarchus of Samos, a Greek philosopher, stated that the Earth went around the Sun in an elliptical orbit. He even calculated that the Sun was about seven times wider (in radius) than the Earth and therefore hundreds of times more voluminous. In 499 CE, about a thousand years before Copernicus, the Indian astronomer Aryabhatta went a step further and propounded that the Earth rotated on its axis, besides going around the Sun. He also predicted solar and lunar eclipses based on his theory.

But it would be a long time before these radical notions displaced the Church's stand on the matter of the Earth's motion.

In medieval Europe, the Church had the authority to suppress anything that went against the Holy Scriptures—including scientific facts. Contradicting the Holy Scriptures was considered heresy, a crime punishable by even torturous death. The Church appointed a group of institutions called the 'Inquisition' to deal with heresy. The Inquisition became responsible for punishing and executing scientists who questioned existing beliefs. Books on subjects that the Inquisition thought contradictory to religious beliefs were banned.

A war between science and religion started brewing, with most of the casualties being on the side of science. Copernicus escaped being punished for heresy only because he died a natural death just as his book was being published.

However, not everyone who defied the Church escaped its wrath.

Almost two hundred years after Copernicus's death, another legendary astronomer and physicist publicly supported the heliocentric theory. Galileo Galilei, born in 1564 in Italy, was renowned even before he began his work in astronomy in 1610. He was the first person to study the simple harmonic motion of a swinging pendulum. He also invented the thermoscope (which later became the thermometer) and the hydrostatic balance, an instrument used for measuring the weight of a body submerged in water. Galileo's good reputation with the religious leaders lasted till the early 1600s, when he came across Copernicus's work (which had been banned for 170 years) and started challenging the geocentric theory.

Since he lived in a country dotted with coastlines, Galileo had ample opportunity to observe the movement of the tides. Every day he would watch the tides rise and fall. Based on his initial work, Galileo believed that the tides were a result of the combined effect of the Earth's revolution and its rotation around the Sun, which created certain forces on the water. Today we know that while Galileo's conclusion about the Earth moving around the Sun was correct, the assumption that tides were caused due to its revolution would be later found to be inaccurate. Tides are caused by the Moon's gravitational pull, as proved by another famous space scientist—Kepler.

In 1610, Galileo started using a telescope to observe other planets like Jupiter and Venus to reaffirm his theory. His work brought him in conflict with the religious leaders of the time, who immediately banned his books and forbade him from sharing his theory with the world.

But Galileo was not to be dissuaded. In 1632, he published a different book on heliocentricity, this time cleverly disguising the theory in a play as a conversation between two people— one advocating heliocentricity and the other in favour of geocentricity. The character supporting the Sun as the centre of the universe was portrayed as a witty scholar while the other was shown as a fool. The play became a roaring success! More importantly, the theory of heliocentricity started gaining momentum.

But Galileo's satire on geocentricity was also taken note of by the leaders of the Church, who were obviously not happy with it. They immediately charged him with heresy. This time, despite his reputation, the Inquisition dealt with him harshly. They threatened him with torture and death unless he publicly withdrew his theory and agreed that the Earth was indeed stationary. Galileo, now an aging man, buckled under pressure. He realized that if he did not concede, he would be burnt at the stake. According to some accounts though, while being forced to apologize for his outrageous theory, Galileo crossed his fingers behind his back as he softly mumbled, '. . . I am apologizing, even as the Earth is still moving.' The Inquisition was not fully satisfied with the apology, and wanted to punish Galileo further. So, they placed him under house arrest for the rest of his life. Renowned artist Cristiano Banti captured this moment in a famous painting which you can see in the image section.

There were many other astronomers who also agreed with the heliocentric theory, but they were all crushed, even as they were slowly starting to gain public favour. It was only after 300 years, in 1820, that the Church allowed another astronomer— Joseph Settle—to finally set things right. The fact that the Sun is indeed the centre of the solar system was finally acknowledged by everyone. In the 1990s, the Vatican acknowledged that the treatment meted out to Galileo had been a mistake. The battle for heliocentricity was finally won.

• • •

Space science is an area which has attracted people for ages. The cavemen would look up at the skies, trying to understand day and night, where clouds came from and how far away the Stars were. They would draw lines and circles around the position of the Stars and determine the shapes they would make. These early men would wonder why the Sun rose every morning and why it disappeared every night. They started relating natural events, life and birth, famines and good harvests, to the position of the Stars. They started thinking of the Stars as heavenly bodies and called them gods. In fact, the Sun was considered a life-giving god by every religion in the world at one point. Daytime was associated with good things like warmth and food, while nights were considered evil and dangerous.

The Future of Space Science

The future of space science is very vibrant. It revolves around three basic questions, which humankind has been asking for centuries:

1. How was the universe born?
2. How can we reach far-off planets, billions of kilometres away?
3. Is there life beyond Earth?

I. How was the universe created?

People have always wondered how the world around them was created. Various religions and tribes have come up with many different theories to answer this question. The Boshongo people of central Africa have a very interesting theory for the origin of the universe. They believe that in the beginning, there was only darkness, water and the great god Bumba. One day Bumba had a stomach ache and vomited out the Sun. The Sun dried up some of the water, leaving the land as we see it today. Still in pain, Bumba vomited out the Moon, the stars and then some animals—the leopard, the crocodile, the turtle and finally, man. Bumba was of course just a part of the imagination of the early Boshongos.

Today, by our best estimates there are around a hundred billion stars in the Milky Way (our galaxy) and at least 140 billion galaxies across the universe. The universe is vast—far beyond our imagination.

Until the twentieth century, we understood almost nothing about the all-important question—how the universe was formed. Then in the 1920s, Edwin Hubble, a famous space scientist in whose name NASA later built the Hubble Telescope, concluded that the universe was not static but always expanding. This also means that if we go back in time, the universe would keep getting smaller and smaller, till the point when it was a mere dot. But this theory sounded irrational to many, and another well-known space scientist, Fred Hoyle, made fun of Hubble by calling his theory 'Big Bang'. Little did he know that in his attempt at mockery, he'd actually end up giving it a name that would go down in history—The Big Bang Theory.

But nobody could prove the Big Bang Theory for the next thirty-five years. Then an accident happened. Space scientists Arno Penzias and Robert Wilson were trying to tune into the high-frequency microwave signals transmitted by our galaxy—the Milky Way or Akash Ganga—when the radio antenna they were using kept picking up a persistent weak hiss of radio noise. They thought the antenna had a problem so they rebuilt it. But the noise persisted. Then it occurred to them that it was probably because of the pigeons in the area or the mess they left on the antennas. So they drove away the pigeons and cleaned the antennas again. Still the hissing continued. After further study they concluded that the hiss they had tried so hard to get rid of was the echo of the Big Bang, which had persisted for billions of years, reverberating across the universe. To get some idea of this, imagine standing on a mountain, where you are surrounded by many other mountains all around you. If you shout, your voice, as a sound wave, will travel, hit other surrounding rocks and then be reflected back at you as another wave. This is called an echo. If there are many mountains and rocks around, you will keep hearing echo after echo, as each of the rocks will keep on reflecting your voice.

Now imagine the Big Bang—it generated waves a trillion times more powerful than your voice. This almost infinite energy travelled as waves and hit the boundaries of the expanding universe.

This echo of the Big Bang was later called Cosmic Microwave Background (CMB) radiation, which is how it is known today.

And that's how the Big Bang Theory came into place. According to this theory, around 13.8 billion years ago, all the matter in the universe emerged from a single minute point, also known as singularity, in a violent burst. This expanded at a very high rate and temperature, doubling in size every 20 to 30 seconds. Within a tiny fraction of a second, gravity and all the other forces were formed. Energy changed into particles of matter and antimatter, which largely destroyed each other. But luckily for us some matter survived, which formed our planet, the solar system and other bodies.

Protons and neutrons started to constitute within the first few seconds. Within minutes these protons and neutrons fused and formed hydrogen and helium nuclei. Even today hydrogen is the most abundant element in the universe.

After 3,00,000 years, groups of protons finally captured electrons to form atoms, filling the universe with clouds of hydrogen and helium gas. After around 3,80,000 years, it left behind a huge train of photons—called the Cosmic Microwave Background that Penzias and Wilson accidentally detected.

So what caused the tiny dot of universe to exist 13.8 billion years ago? We do not know yet.

II. The next-generation spacecraft

On 20 July 1969, the first human team landed on the Moon, creating history. It took *Apollo 11*, the spaceship that carried Neil Armstrong, Michael Collins and Buzz Aldrin, four days, six hours and forty-five minutes to get to the Moon, covering a distance of about 3,80,000 km, at an average speed of 3740 kmph. If we travel with that speed, it would take more than 1.5 years to just reach Mars. Of course, we have more improved technology today than in 1969, with better solid and liquid fuel to burn in order to release the hot gases that thrust the rocket forward.

But even with better fuels, liquid- and- solid- fuelled propulsion has its limitations. It is estimated that it hits a maximum speed of 60,000 kmph. While this is quite fast, it is not even close to the speeds we need to reach the distant planets and stars. The fastest chemically propelled spacecraft created so far, called the *New Horizon*, will reach Pluto in nine years. We cannot even think of sending humans on such long-duration flights!

Clearly, we need systems with greater speed and that require less or no fuel.

Nearly all long-distance spacecraft currently use a feature called the 'gravity assist'. With the help of this feature, the spacecraft do not fly directly to their target planets, but weave around intermediary planets to use their gravity to either increase or decrease their speed with no extra fuel expense. This technology allows current chemical-propelled rockets to hit a speed of up to 62,000 kmph.

A new technology called Ion Propulsion is now being increasingly deployed. Engines with this technology utilize electrical power to charge a gas in a magnetic chamber. Typically, the gas used is xenon. These charged particles, positively-charged atoms, are ejected from the engine to produce thrust. Ion spaceships are not useful for short-distance travel, for instance, to the Moon or Mars, as they take a lot of time to achieve full speed. But they are ideal for long-distance space travel and can hit speeds of up to 3,20,000 kmph. Currently, ion-propelled spaceships are being sent to the Vesta and Ceres asteroids.

Another very promising technology being tested now is that of Solar Sail Spaceships. These are essentially solar-powered spaceships which are light, small and use large solar panels to harness the Sun's energy to power their engines. *Sunjammer* (you can see a photograph of this in the image section), one such spaceship, was launched in late 2014. On the surface, it is just slightly bigger than a washing machine but once deployed in space it expands to thin, large solar sails, about 38m long from end to end. Over long distances, such spaceships can achieve a speed of up to 3,25,000 kmph.

Solar sail is currently where our current prototypes have reached. But could there be faster spaceships in the future? One such possibility is the Laser Beam Spaceship. This is how it works: laser beam, as you may know, is made up of energy particles called photons. In a Laser Beam Spaceship, a large and powerful laser is beamed from a distant place, say the Earth itself. The spaceship accelerates within this beam using energy from the laser (photons). Imagine this as placing a small ball on the top of a pipe carrying water—the water will push the ball forward. Only in this case, the laser beam is far more powerful than the water in the pipe. Space scientists regard this technology as establishing a metro railway network between planets. This technology can even be used for short-distance travel as the acceleration can be very rapid. The maximum speed expected from these Laser Beam Spaceships is about 2 million kmph.

For a long time, another technology which has been considered for spaceships is nuclear propulsion. Nuclear-powered spaceships detonate nuclear fuel in the engine to generate thrust. The only trouble is, such a rocket cannot be powered by fission reaction, our current technology. It needs fusion power, which we are yet to discover despite ongoing efforts in many nations for many decades. Nuclear spaceships, when ready, will be fast, small and ideal for all kinds of travel. It may hit a speed of up to 1,31,000,000 (131 million) kmph, making it possible to reach even distant stars.

TYPE OF SPACESHIP	MAXIMUM SPEED	MOON	MARS	PLUTO	NEAREST STAR SYSTEM (ALPHA CENTAURI)
CHEMICAL POWERED	58,000 kmph	1 day, 8 hours	3 months	10 years	81,500 years
GRAVITY ASSISTED	62,000 kmph	1 day, 8 hours	3 months	9 years 3 months	77,000 years
ION PROPULSION	3,20,000 kmph	2 days	1 month 15 days	2 years 2 months	14,775 years
SOLAR SAIL	3,25,000 kmph	2 days	1 month 12 days	1 year 11 months	14,500 years
LASER BEAM	20,00,000 kmph	4 hours	5 days	3 months 15 days	2360 years
NUCLEAR SPACESHIPS	13,10,00,000 kmph	6 min	2 hours	3 hours	

III. Life on other planets

If there is one question that people never tire of asking space scientists, it is this—is there life outside planet Earth? I remember a fifth-grader, a boy named Ramesh, from Jaunpur, Uttar Pradesh, asking once, 'Sir! When will I be able to shake hands with an alien?' The answer to this question requires some serious thinking.

We all know that so far, despite numerous attempts, no scientist has been able to communicate with or detect life outside the Earth. Of course, the problem may also lie with our communication technologies which, by the standards needed for deep space applications, are still underdeveloped. But a more relevant question to begin with is what makes Earth so conducive to life.

We discussed this with many space scientists and life science experts. Finally, we came up with a list of factors responsible for life on Earth. They are:

1. Its temperature and gravity
2. Its rocky surface
3. The presence of atmosphere
4. The presence of water and oxygen
5. The presence of other greenhouse gases, including carbon dioxide, which keep the planet warm
6. The Moon, which holds the spinning Earth in its position
7. The ozone layer, which cuts off harmful radiation

But are these factors unique to Earth? Out of the trillions of planets in the cosmos, would these conditions be present only on a single planet? We believe that while such conditions are rare indeed, surely there must be many other Earth-like planets.

1. The movement-replicating robot that Dr Kalam tested in Professor Sethu's lab
The robotic hand shown is mirroring the motion of the human hand.

2. Robotic football
In this lab-sized field, each of the two teams, blue and red, had a few players on their side. While one of the robots would assume the role of the attacker, the other would defend the goal. The red team won.

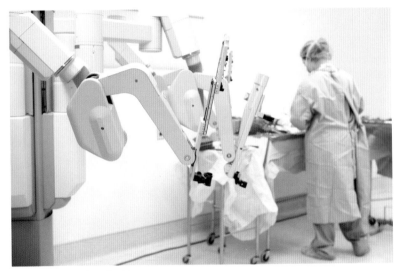

3. The da Vinci Surgical System

4. The SCHAFT robot clearing debris from an entryway

5. Photograph of the first flight by Orville Wright on 17 December 1903
Notice Orville lying flat in the middle of the aircraft. The flight lasted only 12 seconds.

6. Photograph of Orville flying on 4 October 1905
It was amongst the longest flights by the brothers, covering about 40 km in 33 minutes.

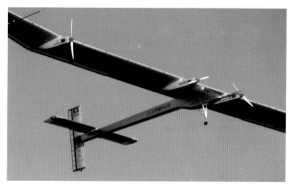

7. *Solar Impulse*, a solar-energy-powered plane which can also fly at night
Though its current maximum speed is only about 80 kmph, it is expected to increase in the future.

8. Cartoon published in 1802 to ridicule Edward Jenner and his work on vaccines
The caption reads—The Cow Pock: The Wonderful Effects of the New Inoculation. It shows people developing cow-like features like horns, hooves, etc. after the vaccination. Jenner is shown in a brown coat, holding the injection syringe.

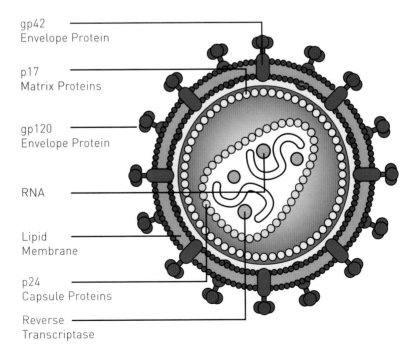

gp42
Envelope Protein

p17
Matrix Proteins

gp120
Envelope Protein

RNA

Lipid
Membrane

p24
Capsule Proteins

Reverse
Transcriptase

9. Anatomy of an AIDS virus

10. Portrait by Cristiano Banti (1857) showing Galileo Galilei facing the Roman Inquisition

11. An artist's impression of the *Sunjammer*, a spaceship with a solar sail

12. Dr Kalam as a young scientist with the legendary scientist and institution builder Dr Vikram Sarabhai

The latter is reviewing a rocket design.

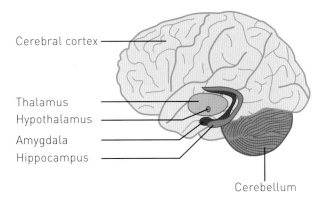

Cerebral cortex

Thalamus
Hypothalamus
Amygdala
Hippocampus

Cerebellum

13. Parts of a human brain

14. The game Mindflex, in which the players use their concentration and thoughts to control the ball

15. Marie Curie, the scientist who pioneered radiation
She was awarded two Nobel Prizes.

16. Rajasaurus, the Indian dinosaur
This is a reconstructed skull of the meat-eating dinosaur that was found at Rahioli, Kheda, Gujarat. It used to live in India about 65 million years ago.

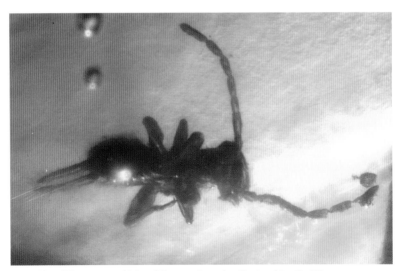

17. A 52-million-year-old fossil insect, found at Vastan Lignite Mine, near Surat, Gujarat
This is one of the best preserved fossils in India.

Let's do some math on this. Say that there are one trillion solar systems in total (there are actually much more than that!).

The Sun is a medium-sized star; about one-third of all stars would be similar in size. So there would be one-third of a trillion, about 3,00,00,00,00,000 solar systems whose Sun is similar to ours.

Of these solar systems, each will have a third planet similar to the Earth in size. Again, the Earth is a medium-sized planet. Assume that about one quarter of all planets are like the Earth. Thus, there will be about 80,00,00,00,000 planets that are almost at equal distance from their suns as the Earth is and are similar in size.

Of these, assume that about 50 per cent have a rocky crust and another 50 percent have atmosphere. So, about 20,00,00,00,000 planets will not only have the size and temperature of the Earth, but also its shape. They will have mountains and air currents too.

Of the ones with atmosphere, we will have to look for those with the right balance of carbon dioxide and oxygen. While carbon dioxide is abundant in the atmosphere, oxygen is relatively rare. Let us assume that about 5 per cent of the remaining planets have them both. That still leaves us with 1,00,00,00,000 (5 per cent of 20 billion) planets with the necessary gas composition.

Of the remaining, about 10 per cent may have water or similar life-giving liquids. That is about 20,0,0,00,000 planets with rocks, clouds and rivers—enough to breed plants and flowers.

For supporting the existence of higher-order animals, these Earth-like planets should also have a single moon, similar to ours, to determine the tides, and more importantly to hold the Earth straight on its axis. About 10 per cent have a single large moon. Hence, about 2,00,00,000 of the Earth-like planets in the universe would have a moon similar to ours.

Finally, the Earth also has certain other critical gases—namely, the greenhouse gases (GHG), besides carbon dioxide, such as methane, which captures heat energy. It also has the ozone layer which protects us from the harmful ultraviolet rays of the Sun. Not more than 1 per cent of the planets would have an ozone layer, or a layer that can effectively reflect UV rays. This still leaves us with about 2,00,000 planets almost identical to the Earth in terms of land, water, Moon, temperature, with almost the same kind of gases and similarly protected from harmful rays. In our estimate, therefore, there are about 2,00,000 earths where life forms are very similar to ours. Some may even have human-like animals with intelligence and the ability to communicate. Some of these planets might have dinosaur-like animals on them while others might only have plants and tiny insects. But one thing is almost certain—life does exist beyond planet the Earth, and some day, with advancing technologies to move into space, a space scientist may indeed shake hands with an alien life form!

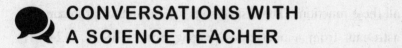

CONVERSATIONS WITH A SCIENCE TEACHER

What is a spacesuit and how is it made?

A spacesuit is a special protective garment worn by humans in outer space. It helps them survive and work in harsh conditions. Remember that astronauts work in zero-pressure vacuum space, and if left exposed, there can be serious damage to the body. The spacesuit also needs to provide a supply of oxygen and eliminate the carbon dioxide that is generated.

There is another problem in outer space—temperature variation. On the Earth, because of convection, the heat is spread out evenly. But in space, the rays of the Sun heat by radiation and thus the temperature can vary by even a hundred degrees, depending on whether an area is under shadow or not. Hence, spacesuits are highly insulated. Additional requirements include shielding against ultraviolet rays and radiation, both of which are abundant in outer space. Sometimes, very small particles called micrometeroids (less than a gram in weight) can be found near the Earth or the Moon. While they are very small, they travel at about 27,000 kmph and hence spacesuits need to be protected against them.

Modern spacesuits have up to eleven different layers for performing all these functions. These spacesuits are capable of protecting the astronaut from temperatures ranging from –156 °C (–249 °F) to 121 °C. The complete cost of a spacesuit is about $11 million although 70 per cent of this is for the backpack and the control module. They allow oxygen for up to eight hours of spacewalk.

Spacesuits are very heavy, but that does not matter—everything is weightless in outer space. However, we will need lightweight spacesuits when we land on Mars, because it has gravity, just like the Earth.

What is a light year?

Distances in space are not measured in kilometres; they are calculated in units called light years. One light year is the distance light can travel in vacuum in a year's time. Now since light travels 3,00,000 km in a single second, one light year is about 9,50,00,00,00,00,000 km (95 followed by 11 zeroes or 95 trillion). Now that is a huge distance indeed, but by universal standards, it is not a lot. Say we have a space vehicle that can travel at the speed of light. It would still take us about four years to leave the solar system and reach the nearest star, the Alpha Centauri

Star System. And it would take us 25,000 years, travelling at the speed of light, to check out of our galaxy, the Milky Way, and reach Canis Major Dwarf Galaxy, our nearest galaxy.

How big is the universe and what is its shape?

We are not really sure of the size and shape of the universe. For all practical purposes, the universe is infinite. In fact, the size of the universe would depend on its shape. Some scientists believe it is spherical. If that is so, then the radius of this sphere should be around 92 billion light years. But recent conclusions of NASA suggest that the universe is almost flat with a very small curvature, which make it infinite.

I have heard there are many asteroids and meteors flying around the universe. Do they not endanger the Earth?

On any given day the Earth is showered with about 20,000 meteorites above one kg in weight. But our planet has a unique protection against these meteors—its atmosphere. The moment a foreign particle enters the Earth's atmosphere, it compresses the air in front of it. When air is compressed it heats up and soon its temperature goes up to 1650 degrees centigrade. This combined with the effect of frictional heating burns up the foreign object, converting it to dust and ash—which falls safely on the Earth as gravel—about 100 tons every day!

But the next generation of space scientists cannot just rely on the atmosphere to burn up the asteroids which crash into the Earth. Sixty-six million years ago, a very large asteroid entered the atmosphere. Because of its size it didn't get completely burnt up. It hit the Earth near Mexico as a ten-kilometre-wide rock and nearly wiped out all the major life forms on the Earth, including the dinosaurs. So space scientists are already exploring ways in which such large and unwanted asteroids can be diverted with human effort. There are three courses of action we can take in such an event.

The first and perhaps the most effective method would be to use a gravity tug. We will have to send a robotic probe on a spaceship to meet the asteroid in outer space. The robotic spaceship will move closely with the asteroid itself. The spacecraft's small gravity will exert a little pull on the asteroid as the two move through space together. Over months or perhaps even years, this 'gravity pull' method will pull the asteroid into a different, safer orbit away from the Earth.

But in some cases there might not be enough time to react or the asteroid might be too large to pull by gravity. In such an event we will have to ram the spaceship right into the asteroid, destroying it and thereby pushing the asteroid away from the Earth.

The last option is to try and blow up the asteroid itself. This is something you might see in movies, though space scientists believe this to be a method with unsure results. It will need a few nuclear bombs which will have to be carried by a spaceship and detonated over the asteroid. But we cannot be sure how many pieces it will blow up into or where those pieces will go.

What is dark energy and dark matter?

Till 1990 the general belief amongst space scientists was that the universe is expanding, but the rate of expansion is slowing down with time due to the force of gravity. However, in 1998, the famous Hubble Space Telescope observed a faraway supernova whose characteristics showed that the universe was actually expanding faster now. This observation changed the prevailing theory completely.

Now if the universe is expanding, there has to be some force causing this. Scientists have called this force Dark Energy. Unfortunately, that is all we know about it. It is spread throughout space, and surprisingly, 70 per cent of the universe is made up of this dark energy.

But dark energy is not the only huge unknown force in the universe. The universe is made of stars, planets, comets and many other such bodies. They absorb, reflect or emit light. This is the visible matter. However, when space scientists calculated the gravity experienced by these visible matter bodies, it was much more than expected. This suggested that there were invisible bodies of matter in the universe which were pulling them. Since we know nothing about them except the fact that such matter exists, it was called Dark Matter. Surprisingly, when space scientists calculated the expected amount of dark matter, it turned out that it outweighed visible matter by a factor of 6 to 1. Hence, while the visible matter, including all the stars, planets, suns and comets, makes up about 4 per cent of the universe, dark matter makes up about 96 per cent of the total universe.

It is indeed going to be a challenge for future space scientists to unravel the mysteries of this 96 per cent.

We discussed the expansion of space. How fast is it really happening?

In a nutshell, space is expanding rapidly. In the language of the space scientists, it is 74.2 kilometres per second per megaparsec. Let us understand this.

Megaparsec is a unit of distance used to measure space distance. One megaparsec, 1 Mpc, is about 3 million light years of distance (about 3 followed by 20 zeroes kilometres). Now, imagine you are standing on the Earth and observing a distant planet called 'Alpha', which is exactly 1 Mpc away from you. Due to the expansion of the universe it would be moving away from you at a rate of 74.2 kilometres every second. Now, let's say you set your observation on another planet called 'Beta' which is 5 Mpc away from you. This planet would be moving away from you at a rate of 74.2 x 5 = 371 kilometres every second. The farther the planet is, the faster it is moving away from us, because of the expansion of the universe.

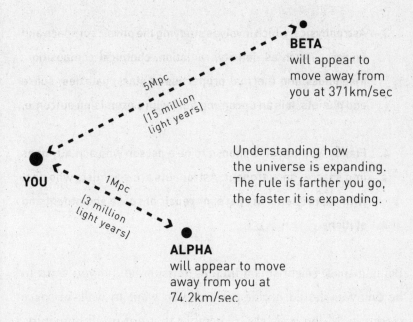

BETA
will appear to move away from you at 371km/sec

5Mpc
(15 million light years)

YOU

1Mpc
(3 million light years)

Understanding how the universe is expanding. The rule is farther you go, the faster it is expanding.

ALPHA
will appear to move away from you at 74.2km/sec

How can I become a space scientist?

There are multiple fields within space science one can choose to pursue.

Broadly, there are four major career streams:

1. Traditional astronomy, which is the study of stars, planets, galaxies, etc.

2. Astronautics, which is about designing the next generation of spaceships, understanding space environment, space food and designing spacesuits

3. Astrophysics, which involves studying the physics of space and universe, such as density, radiation, chemical composition, mechanics and thermal properties of stars, galaxies, space and planets. It is an upcoming field with a promising outcome.

4. Finally, you can also choose to be a person who actually goes into space—an astronaut. Astronauts are scientists who deal with experiments in space, or repair of space equipment and stations.

Being a space scientist is a lifelong mission, and if you want to be one you should decide early. If you want to walk in space or on the Moon or Mars, remember that out of all humanity, so far only about 550 people have been to space. It is a very competitive career. Also, if you want to be considered a potential spacewalker, you must maintain excellent health. Space is a hostile environment and only the fittest can survive in it. So it is important that you stay fit and focused.

Fortunately, India is a nation with a very strong space research programme and associated training. The Indian Institute of Space Sciences and Technology (IIST) offers comprehensive programmes in space science and most of its graduates find employment in leading space organizations like ISRO. There are many other universities in India and abroad that offer similar programmes, such as the University of North Dakota's Department of Space Studies which offers programmes up to PhD in the study of asteroids and development of other planets such as Mars for inhabitation.

 ## MEET THE EXPERT: Dr A.P.J. ABDUL KALAM

Dr A.P.J. Abdul Kalam is the expert in this section being interviewed by Srijan on various dimensions of his experience as a space scientist. Dr Kalam, who started his career in aeronautics in 1960, served for almost two decades in this field. He was the project director of India's first indigenous Satellite Launch Vehicle (SLV-III), which successfully deployed the Rohini satellite near the Earth's orbit in July 1980. He is being interviewed here by the co-author Srijan Pal Singh here.

Q. How were you inspired to pursue a career in space science?

My father used to repair boats for a living. I would often accompany him when he took the boats into the sea to test them. This was the late 1930s, when I was about seven or eight years old. Since most fishermen wanted their boats ready by the morning, sometimes my father had to work through the night. In Rameshwaram, back then, the skies at night were mostly clear. One could see millions of tiny dots of light sprayed across those skies from the seashores and the boats. Even as a child I was fascinated by the skies . . . and space. I remember one of my primary school teachers, the great Sri Sivasubramaniam Iyer, telling the class once how to distinguish between a star and a planet—stars twinkle and planets do not. The warm and cold air belts in the atmosphere were responsible for this effect. From that day onwards, whenever I looked at the night skies, I would carefully separate the planets from the stars—the stars were always so much more in number!

My fascination with space met with a purpose when I joined the Indian Space Research Organization (ISRO) in the 1960s. Back then, ISRO had just started out under the vision of its founder, Dr Vikram Sarabhai. It was a glorious thing for a nation that had just freed itself from foreign slavery. Many people questioned the wisdom of putting money into space research. Did India really have the resources to compete against other (far richer) space-faring countries?

Q. Fifty years ago, when you started your work in space science, the technological environment was very different. I am sure there would have been many difficulties when India started its space mission. Can

you share some incident highlighting those problems and how you and your team overcame them?

I remember the difficulties we faced in establishing an organization whose purpose was understood only by a handful of the population. In the early 1960s, Professor Vikram Sarabhai, with his team, located a place technically most suited for space research after considering many alternatives. The place, Thumba in Kerala, was selected for space research as it was near the magnetic equator, and was ideal for ionospheric and electrojet research in the upper atmosphere.

Acquiring that area for our purpose was a huge challenge for Professor Sarabhai. He approached the Kerala government administrators first. After surveying the profile of the land and the coastline, we found that the place was inhabited by thousands of fishing folk. It also had an ancient St Mary Magdalene Church, the Bishop's House and a school. Acquiring this land was going to be very difficult indeed. So many people would have to be relocated. And what about the important institutions that stood there? While most of the administrative officials barely understood the potential usage of the land, thanks to Vikram Sarabhai's reputation, they were at least willing to provide land in an alternative area. But Professor Sarabhai was in a predicament which neither politicians nor administrators could understand. The location of Thumba was unique, and any alternative would hugely undermine the space research.

After much debate and discussion, somebody suggested we approach the only person who could possibly advise and help—Reverend Father Peter Bernard Pereira, the bishop of the region. Professor Sarabhai approached the bishop on a Saturday evening. As a junior scientist, I accompanied him. The meeting between the two turned out to be historical.

Reverend Father exclaimed, 'Oh Vikram, you are asking for my children's abode, my abode and God's abode. How is it possible?' Then he fell into deep thought.

Father Pereira finally asked Professor Sarabhai to come to church the following Sunday at 9 in the morning.

Professor Sarabhai went to the church with his team again on Sunday. At that time Father Pereira was reading out from the Bible. After the prayer, the bishop invited Professor Sarabhai to the dais and introduced him to the people with a speech which remains as clear in my mind as it was when it was delivered five decades ago: 'Dear children, here is a scientist, Professor Vikram Sarabhai. What do the sciences do? All of us experience, including this church, the light from electricity. I am able to talk to you through this microphone, which is made possible by technology. The diagnosis and treatment given to patients by doctors come from medical science. Science through technology enhances the comfort and quality of human life. What do I do, as a preacher? I pray for you, for your well-being, for your peace. In short, what Vikram is doing and what I am doing are the same—both science and spirituality seek the Almighty's blessings for human prosperity. Dear children, Professor Vikram says that he will build within a year, near the coast, alternative facilities to what we have. Now dear children, can we give your abode, can we give my abode, can we give God's abode for a great scientific mission?' There was pin-drop silence. Then everyone got up and said 'Amen', making the whole church reverberate.

That church became our design centre, where we started rocket assembly, and the bishop's house served as a workplace for our scientists. Later, the Thumba Equatorial Rocket Launching Station (TERLS) led to the establishment of the Vikram Sarabhai Space Centre (VSSC). The space research activities transformed into multiple space centres throughout the country. Now this church has become an important centre of learning, where thousands of people come to know about the dynamic history of the space programme in India. Of course, the Thumba citizens received well-equipped facilities, a place for worship and an educational centre in an alternate place.

Professor Vikram Sarabhai and Rev. Peter Bernard Pereira may not be with us anymore, but their work, which has been instrumental in the birth of India's space missions, truly lives on.

NOTE TO PARENTS

Space science is a highly exciting field which will only see more growth in the future. In the next ten to fifteen years, we will be sending more people into space and other planets, harnessing solar energy from space and maybe even starting space tourism! Perhaps we will also set up a centralized and concentrated effort to establish countermeasures against asteroids and man-made space junk. In the face of these events, there is bound to be a strong demand for space scientists and astronauts.

India is emerging as one of the top space-faring nations in the world—a position we are likely to hold on to with ISRO's continuing success. Space scientists from India are in demand at the global level. IIST conducts a highly subsidized programme in space science which is offered on merit through a competitive exam—the first of its kind in the world.

OATH FOR THE ASPIRING SPACE SCIENTIST

'As a great space scientist, I will be remembered for unravelling the mysteries of the universe, discover how the universe was born or invent spaceships with which humankind can travel deep into space or establish first contact with extraterrestrial life.'

(Write this oath in the space below. You can also add new thoughts and goals for yourself.)

_____

_____

_____

_____

_____

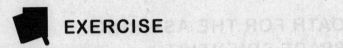

EXERCISE

Remember the discussion we had earlier in this chapter regarding how to protect the Earth from asteroids? Something interesting actually happened in 2014 in this area. Space scientists successfully managed to land a rover on a moving comet. This was called the Rosetta mission. Go and read more about it. Can you find the name of the comet, the name of the lander and other details about them? Write a small two-hundred-word report on this.

1 A Brief Note on Religious Objections to Copernicus. http://www.astronomy. ohio-state.edu/~pogge/Ast161/Unit3/ response.html

2 Hawking, Stephen. 2003. *On the Shoulders of Giants: The Great Works of Physics and Astronomy*. Penguin UK

CHAPTER 5

In 2011, as part of an assignment we travelled halfway across the world to Boston, USA. Boston, along with the metropolitan area of Greater Boston, is a vibrant city with about 45 lakh people and one of the oldest districts in the United States. What makes it unique is the fact that it is home to some of the finest universities in the world—including Harvard University and the Massachusetts Institute of Technology. These institutions have produced some of the finest scientific minds in the world; in fact, more than 150 Nobel laureates have been associated with Harvard alone. The university is also part of the prestigious Ivy League group of educational institutions which comprise eight prominent universities in the United States.

On a pleasant day in September, upon finishing our assignment earlier than expected, we decided to take a stroll along Oxford Street, a beautiful walkway lined with colourful trees. There we came across the Center for Brain Science, which is one of the world's leading institutions for brain and neurological research. Excited, we decided to go inside.

The first neuroscientist we met was Professor Bobby Kasthuri, a leading researcher in the Lichtman Laboratory. A young professor with a thick beard and long, thin spectacles, he showed us a presentation on his latest work in understanding the human brain. He said, 'Much of our work is in understanding the working of neurons and synapses. We want to understand how the brain develops.'

Neurons, the building blocks or primary cells which make up the brain and the entire nervous system, are spread all over the body, but of course are highly concentrated in the brain itself. The presence of neurons is unique to animals, as plants do not have them.

Now, for every action and its subsequent reaction, neurons have a major role to play. They act as 'messengers'. For instance, if you touch a hot surface, the neurons at your fingertips pass on the information to the nearby neurons and this continues till the information ultimately reaches the brain. The brain then processes this information and generates a command for your hand muscles to move the finger away. This again happens through the same channel of neurons. Neurons have special sites called synapses, from which information is transmitted from one neuron to another. Imagine a synapse as a small gap with transmitters, much like an electrical outlet, where another neuron can plug into its synapse, which acts as a receptor. One neuron can have a large number of such synapses, so it can communicate in all directions. The human brain has about 100 billion neurons and quadrillion synapses. This makes understanding the human brain a truly complicated assignment.

Coming back to Professor Kasthuri and his presentation at the Brain Research Center, we were made to sit in front of a large screen inside the meeting room. Before starting, the professor clarified to us, 'Much of our work is currently limited to understanding the brain of a rat. It is far less complicated and hence relatively easier to understand. Once we have achieved this, we hope to replicate the same for the human brain.'

Professor Kasthuri then showed us a picture of a very special equipment—a nano knife made of diamond. He said, 'We take the brain of a dead rat. Then we use the nano knife to cut slices less than 30 nanometres long. In this way, a single brain generates hundreds of thousands of slices.'

He continued, 'But that is not the difficult task. We can make about 2500 slices in a single day. The real task begins after this.

Each of these slices is labelled and then placed under an electron microscope. We store this as a digital image in a computer.'

Can you guess how large this data from a single rat brain would be? It would need more than one petabyte of storage to preserve digital images of the rat's brain. This is equal to storing about 40 billion photos! Now, once these photographs are ready, Professor Kasthuri and his team map specific neurons in these images to observe their pattern and dynamics. It is like a colour-coded map showing neurons in the brain. In this way, they can study any specific neuron in a rat's brain.

When we went back to the hotel after this meeting, our heads were full of ideas and questions. We were thinking what if we were to scale Professor Kasthuri's experiment to understand the human mind. We then spent some time analysing the neural patterns of different animals. The results are shown below:

NAME OF SPECIES	TOTAL NUMBER OF NEURONS IN THE ENTIRE NERVOUS SYSTEM1
Roundworm	300
Jellyfish	800
Snail	11,000
Fruit fly	1,00,000
Ant	2,50,000
Honeybee	9,50,000
Frog	1,60,00,000
Rat	20,00,00,000
Octopus	30,00,00,000
Human	86,00,00,00,000[2]

Notice that the humans have almost 430 times the number of neurons as that of a rat. It would take years to fully map a single human brain, and one would need supercomputers far more powerful than the ones we have today. Further, it is estimated that to map an entire human brain, it would take about 500 petabytes of data, about five times the memory space used by Facebook to store the information of its one billion accounts worldwide! That's not all—the hard drives needed to store the neural map of a single human brain would occupy an entire building of fifteen storeys. The human brain is indeed the most complicated gift of evolution. Understanding this complex network of neurons and synapses is the ultimate challenge for any neuroscientist.

The human brain, though complicated, is also a well-evolved organ of the body. The brain has gone through multiple stages of evolution as we have evolved from reptiles to mammals and then to advanced intelligent forms—human beings. In fact this is represented in the human brain itself. It can be imagined as consisting of three different layers, one on top of the other. The oldest and innermost layer is called the reptilian brain and it contains the brain stem (connecting to the spinal cord), the cerebellum and other parts where our brain is similar to reptiles. These control basic functions like the heartbeat, lungs, digestion, blood pressure, etc. This part of the brain evolved 500 million years ago.

The next layer is called *mammalian brain* and it evolved as we transformed into mammals from reptiles. It is located just above the reptilian brain and consists of something called the limbic system, which involves emotions, basic memory and sorting ability, say to determine friend and foe. It consists of:

- **the hippocampus,** where short-term memories are converted into long-term memories
- **the amygdala,** a small almond-shaped part of the brain which governs emotions, especially fear
- **the thalamus,** which acts as a relay station, gathering all sensory information like sight, sound, touch, smell and taste, and transmits it to the various parts of the brain and
- **the hypothalamus,** which regulates body temperature (remember reptiles are cold-blooded, but mammals are warm-blooded with their body temperature being constant)

But what separates us from other mammals is the third and outermost layer of the brain—the **cerebral cortex.** In the typical brain diagram or model, the curvy portion with folds is nothing but the cerebral cortex. It is so folded and curved that it is able to pack itself into the skull easily despite the fact that it has a larger area. It is like a 2-millimetre-thick sheet folded into multiple layers. Typically, the cerebral cortex is also called the **grey matter,** which lends intelligence and memory. It makes up for about 80 per cent of the weight of the brain and controls most of the functions of memory, sensory data, speech, understanding languages, making decisions, controlling most of the motion of body, etc. (A diagram of the parts of the brain is shown in the image section.)

The brain essentially works on electromagnetic signals, which means it has electrical and magnetic signals running through it all the time, similar to a mobile phone or any other electronic device, but of course of a very different frequency and properties. When you think or see or try to remember something, the thousands of neurons inside the brain rapidly exchange information with each other leading to a surge—like waves in an ocean as they are 'fired' one after the other. The waves in an ocean are quite slow, about ten seconds per wave, or one-tenth cycle per second. The brain wave can be quite rapid, anything between 10 to 100 cycles per second. (Comparatively, a mobile phone using radio waves has a faster wave cycle, about 200 million cycles per second.) It is these brain waves which allow different parts of the brain to communicate with each other, thereby helping us to make decisions.

For instance, imagine a scenario where you are batting in a game of cricket. The bowler hurls a ball at you from twenty-two yards, which would take less than one second to reach the batsman. During that time, you have seen the ball, analysed its path for any swing or spin, determined where it would bounce off the ground, predicted its further path and then moved your hands and legs (along with the bat) to hit the ball at a given angle. Of course, while doing all this, you have also factored

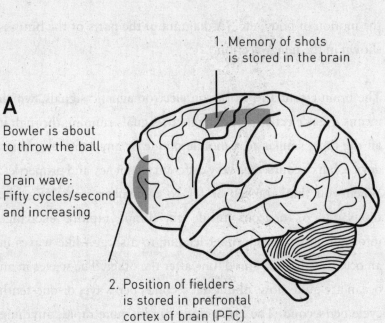

A

Bowler is about
to throw the ball

Brain wave:
Fifty cycles/second
and increasing

1. Memory of shots
is stored in the brain

2. Position of fielders
is stored in prefrontal
cortex of brain (PFC)

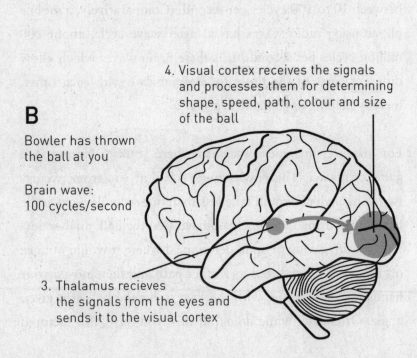

B

Bowler has thrown
the ball at you

Brain wave:
100 cycles/second

4. Visual cortex receives the signals
and processes them for determining
shape, speed, path, colour and size
of the ball

3. Thalamus recieves
the signals from the eyes and
sends it to the visual cortex

7. Anterior Cirgulate Cortex (ACC) determines the rewards (runs which will be potentially scored)

C

Brain wave: 100 cycles/second

Ball is about to reach you and you must decide what to do

5. Orbitofrontal Cortex (OFC) decides the shot to play. OFC fetches information about fielders from PFC

6. Amygdala determines any motion and reflex, like ducking the ball

8. Cerebellum controls different parts of the body, like hands and legs to play the shot

D

Playing the shot

Brain wave: 100 cycles/second and reducing

9. Spinal cord transmits the signals from the cerebellum to respective body parts

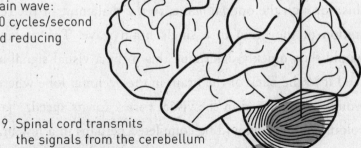

in the memory of the fielders and the runs you want to make from the shot. All this sounds complicated, doesn't it? But when you play cricket, this seems effortless. Let us see how this information actually transmits through the brain and on to other neurons in the body.

To begin with, even before the ball is bowled, you would have looked around the field to see the fielders' positions and also remembered the rate of scoring needed for your team to win. The visual positioning of fielders is stored as a short-term memory in the prefrontal cortex of your brain. Of course, the long-term memory of what shots to play to which kind of ball is already stored in your long-term memory all over the cerebral cortex (outer layer) of the brain. At this stage, your brain waves would be about 40–50 cycles per second.

Then when the bowler throws the ball at you, your brain waves increase rapidly to up to 100 cycles per second. First, the neurons in your eyes, situated in the retina, will process the images of the balls continuously and keep transmitting this, through the optical nerve, to the thalamus, or the relay station of the brain in a single brain wave. The thalamus would then quickly determine this to be a visual signal and send it to the back of the brain in the occipital lobe where it would be processed in the visual cortex for its speed, shape, colour, etc. This would be completed perhaps in a few brain waves.

In the next few brain cycles, the occipital lobe will transmit the processed information to many parts of the brain. It will go towards the front outer layer of the brain, in the orbitofrontal cortex (OFC) which makes decisions on what shot to play. It will also go to the amygdala, located in the middle of the brain, which controls emotional reactions such as reflexes. The same information will also go to the anterior cingulate cortex (ACC), above the amygdala, which determines rewards (how many runs can you get for a particular shot selected). This may take many cycles, as different rewards may come up for different shots and the final selection would be based on the best possible reward.

Once the selection is finally made, the next step is to signal the muscles in your body, especially the hands and legs, to move in order to execute the shot. This again takes a few cycles of brain waves. This is controlled by multiple parts of the brain. In the case of generating motion, besides the front of the brain, a significant role is played by the cerebellum, located at the very back of the brain below the ears. Cerebellum controls balance, posture and equilibrium.

After this the neural signal travels down the spinal cord along the backbone into the respective body parts which make the muscles move. In case the ball changes the trajectory and there is a need to determine a new shot, the complete cycle may be repeated.

This is the reason why it is difficult to play a very fast ball and also a ball which turns and spins a lot. In case of a rapidly travelling ball, the brain is unable to process and determine a reaction within the 100-cycles-per-second limit. In case of a turning and spinning ball, the brain has to reprocess the decision-making again and again because of the changing path of the ball.

• • •

In 2014, we had another unique experience in the field of neural sciences. This time it was in Scotland, at the Ann Rowling Regenerative Neurology Clinic. This clinic is situated in the beautiful city of Edinburgh. Ann Rowling Clinic is funded by J.K. Rowling, the bestselling author of the Harry Potter series, in memory of her mother, Anne, who died at the age of forty-five due to multiple sclerosis, a neural disorder where the neurons degenerate. J.K. Rowling set out on a mission to eradicate multiple sclerosis and, along with it, many other diseases of the brain.

On a sunny afternoon in May, we reached the clinic after an hour-long drive from our hotel. The clinic is part of the research network of the University of Edinburgh. The clinic is a single-storey building, with large glass walls which make it sunny and thus saves electricity. As we got down from our car, we were greeted by Professor Siddharthan Chandran, who is the director of the clinic. He is also amongst the world's most renowned neurologists. Professor Chandran showed us the different scientific experiments they were working on. The striking thing about the Ann Rowling Regenerative Neurology Clinic is that it is not only a research facility but also a treatment centre.

We were particularly impressed by the work being conducted in the field of early detection of mental and neural disorders. Neurons are perhaps the most complicated of cells, and it is these complications that affect their functionalities. The first step towards the treatment of neural disorders therefore is to identify the problem as early as possible.

Professor Chandran demonstrated his work on deploying technologies typically used by eye-care professionals to help detect neural disorders. The device is similar to the one that an optometrist uses on you, when they ask you to place your chin on a particular rest and then use a telescope-like equipment to look into your eyes and ask you to identify objects and their clarity.

Using similar optical scanning devices his team can map the inside of the eye, particularly the retina, where light from the outer eye is finally converted into images. But Professor Chandran is going further and targeting the optical nerve. This is a small opening in the retina which carries neurons and photoreceptors from the eye to the brain. Imagine it like a data cable which carries images from the retina to the inner brain. These optical nerves, from both the eyes, carry data at the speed of 10 Mbps (Megabits per second), which is about twenty times the average broadband speed we use to surf the Internet! Now as you would imagine, the optical nerve is full of millions of neurons to transmit such a large amount of data, for about sixteen hours every day when we are awake. Using advanced technologies they are able to 'peep' down the optical nerves using the special retina scanners for new millimetres and make a longitudinal and cross-sectional image of it (front-facing and sideways images). Now these images can either show smooth nerve patterns, with one neuron over another indicating the good health of the neurons or distortions, that is, variations in the thickness of the neuron layers indicating the beginning of neuron decay. If such a symptom is observed, the patient is immediately put under medical care to stop the decay and regrow the lost neurons. Such an analysis and early detection can be done at extremely low costs and in a matter of minutes, and hence expected to help patients worldwide. It also shows how eye care and brain care are converging to provide better health care for humanity.

The Future of Neuroscience

Neuroscience will essentially progress in three directions in the future. First it can help understand the human brain itself, which can even lead to better computers. Secondly, it can help deal with the ailments of the neural systems; the current methods are quite nascent and many neural disorders are still beyond treatment. The third area will emerge in the field of creating bridges between the human brain and machines and perhaps one day, between one brain and another. Let us explore this further.

The human brain is the most difficult organ to understand. We are still miles away from fully comprehending how it works, how thoughts come to us, how memories are created and how we make decisions. The brain is even more complicated because while it is made up of proteins, the building block of neurons; it also exhibits electromagnetic properties. Understanding the brain will help us evolve new methods of learning. It might someday perhaps be even possible to download data and information directly on to the brain—enabling years of education to be transferred to the brain within a matter of minutes! In fact, there has already been some progress in this direction at the University of California, where a group of neuroscientists have made it possible to video record the thoughts and imagination of a person. They begin by showing the subject a large number of videos and images and recording the electromagnetic signals generated in the brain when the viewing is happening. Then they map these signals to visual elements such as colour, texture, shape, etc. as seen by the person. Of course, that means mapping millions and millions of data sets from a single person. Once a map has been created, one can recreate any image from the brain signals. The trick is, even when you imagine a photo, almost the same areas of the brain work as those when you actually see the photo. Hence, if you are then asked to imagine a painting of a flower, your visual cortex will start working and then the MRI (an instrument used to measure the brain's electromagnetic activity) will pick up the corresponding brain signals and send it to the computer. The computer matches the signals with the existing database and reconstructs the image. Such reconstructed images are quite accurate, though there is scope for improvement. If this works, then in the future the other way round will also work, which means you send electromagnetic signals to the brain and it will construct images without the need of eyes. Imagine, computers could simply read your thoughts then, you could store your memories on a hard disk and most importantly, people suffering from visual impairment could be made to see without the need of eyes at all!

The second future area of application of neurosciences would be to deal with the ailments of the neural systems. The brain, as we all know, is a highly protected organ of the body, located in the cranium. It is well supplied with oxygen; almost 20 per cent of the total blood and oxygen circulated in the body goes to the brain, making it the highest priority organ of the human body. Brain cells hence have considerably longer lifespans compared to other cells. But there is a catch—we are born with almost all the brain cells, which is about 100 billion neurons. Hardly any brain cells are added after birth, and so the human body is hardly capable of replacing ageing and dead brain cells. Cells once lost in the brain, especially the cerebral cortex, can never be replaced. Up until the 1900s, the average lifespan of humans was about thirty-five to forty years and hence the irreplaceability of the brain cells was never an issue. But from the middle of the twentieth century, thanks to advances in medical sciences, the human lifespan has seen considerable increase. For instance, a person born in Japan today can expect to live up to eighty-eight years! Even the global average is about seventy-one years. This increase of lifespan has posed a new challenge to neural sciences—that of age-related degeneration of brain cells, which unlike other organs just cannot be replaced.

The most prominent of these ailments is Alzheimer's disease (AD). AD mostly occurs in people over sixty-five years of age—when the brain loses the ability to store short-term memories and so the patient keeps forgetting things they have done or people they have met in the last five to ten minutes. Eventually, it leads to long-term memory loss as well, with patients forgetting their relatives, languages and even basic functions like swallowing and breathing. There are about three crore cases of Alzheimer's disease currently, most of them in the higher age groups. Alzheimer's is predicted to affect one in 85 people globally by 2050, making it the most costly disease to society. So far, there is no cure for Alzheimer's disease and many other neural disorders. This is the challenge for the next generation of neuroscientists—to find ways to replace human brain cells. Some work in this direction has already begun. On one hand there is an effort to develop medicines which can strengthen neurons and their ability to live longer lifespans; on the other hand, something truly unique is being attempted. We saw in the Ann Rowling clinic in Scotland how there is a very promising scientific research being conducted around actually growing neural cells from stem cells itself. In the future, these neurons, grown in Petri dishes, could be replaced in the ageing brain—but of course we are at least 10–15 years away from this becoming a reality. The challenge is also to accurately pinpoint which cell to place in which location of the brain.

Now we come to the third area, which is truly exciting and a bridge between engineering and anatomy. On the face of it, it looks like a work of science fiction. Since the discovery of fire and wheel, humans have mastered the ability to control machines; today we can do all our daily activities, cooking, eating, reading, typing, brushing, industrial applications, transport and virtually anything you can think of with the help of machines. These machines are controlled by our hands and fingers and, in some cases, like the accelerator of car, with the help of legs and feet too. However, modern neuroscientists consider this whole process of controlling machines with limbs an inefficient exercise, as it limits us to using only a certain number of devices with our limited limbs and fingers. Also, this method is slow and those individuals, whose mobility is restricted, are severely deterred in their ability to use machines. So what is the next-generation control mechanism?

It is called *Brain Machine Interface*. Sometime back, Srijan purchased a new test toy from Amazon's online market. It was a neatly packed device called Mindflex. (You can see a picture of this in the image section.) We were surprised to see how the game worked. Mindflex is rated amongst the most innovative products in the market today. It consists of a set of hoops and baskets and a small light ball, which can be lifted on a cushion of air using a set of fans under it. The ball appears to rise in the air, and by controlling the flow of air you can make it go back and forth to cross the hoops and the baskets. But the tricky and the innovative part is how you control the fan's air speed. It is controlled by the power of your concentration! Mindflex comes with an electromagnetic sensor headset which has to be attached around the user's head, and it measures the intensity of brain waves. Remember, brain waves are electromagnetic in nature, and the more you concentrate the stronger they will be. The complex electromagnetic sensor in Mindflex detects and measures these waves and then uses their intensity to control the power on the fan, which in turn controls the ball. So, the ball actually moves around depending on what and how hard you are thinking. Srijan and I were both enthralled by the first level of the brain machine direct interface. It is merely the tip of the iceberg.

The brain machine interface is already seeing new dimensions, and we were first-hand witnesses to it. In 2011, we went to Australia to attend a series of events. One day, we visited the University of Technology, Sydney, popularly called UTS.

This is one of the largest universities of science and engineering the world over and is well known for its department of biomechanical engineering. There we met Professor Hung Nyugen, a global expert on robotics, biomechanics and artificial intelligence. He showed us a unique project which he was working on with some PhD students, funded by the Motor Accident Authority of Australia. Their challenge was to help patients who are permanently brain damaged from accidents, and hence have no control over their bodies. These patients can think and have perfectly normal brain activity, but because of the injury in their motor nerves, they are left paralysed. The professor explained to us how his team was studying brain waves to detect the exact signals that the brain generates when it thinks of various motions—going forward, backwards, left and right, slow and fast. They found these signals remarkably different from each other. The signals can be distinguished with a strong electromagnetic sensor, and this discovery became the key to their work. They started working on a special wheelchair, whose motors were controlled by a regulator attached to a brain wave sensor. He showed us the wheelchair, which looked like any ordinary wheelchair with motors, but with no control panel and thick cap which had to be worn by the operator. One of his students enthusiastically volunteered to give us a demo and sat in the chair and put on the electromagnetic cap. Another student switched on the chair, which had a toggle switch. Soon the operator in the chair, without touching anything, started thinking to himself, 'I must go forward, I want to go forward.'

And the chair slowly started rolling ahead. Then the operator started thinking about stopping the motion, and the chair stopped. Like this, we saw him turn the chair around, go back, move in angles and navigate to the door—without moving a single muscle—all with the power of thoughts. Finally, Professor Nyugen looked at us and laughed. 'Thoughts are powerful,' he summed up. Professor Nyugen told us that he was now working on a car which could be controlled by thoughts alone, but of course he could not show its working. He said, 'I am sure the car will work, but currently the traffic police does not allow mind-driven cars!' We all laughed and were happy to see how the neurosciences are already converging with robotics and mechanics to help humanity.

 ## CONVERSATIONS WITH A SCIENCE TEACHER

What is the capacity of the human memory?

One of the most remarkable abilities of the human brain is the large capacity of its long-term memory, stored mostly in the prefrontal cortex. We are not really sure of the size of this memory, but it is widely accepted that the capacity of the human memory is about 2500 terabytes. To understand this, imagine a standard hard disk—it stores about 0.5 to 1 terabyte of data. Similarly, the human brain is able to store data of about 5000 hard disks. If the complete data from an adult human brain is burnt on DVDs, it would require as many as twenty-seven lakh discs.

How are memories created?

In the last five years there has been some research done in this area, but it is still not fully understood how memories are created. Yet what is known is that the brain is divided into two kinds of memories—the short term and the long-term memory.

Information enters the brain through the five senses. It is the thalamus which then sends it to various parts of the brain to process it (for example, all sights are processed by the visual cortex). The processed information is then sent to the front part of the brain—prefrontal cortex—and enters into the conscious. This is called the short-term memory. But short-term memory lasts only for a few minutes.

Sometimes, it is necessary to remember things for a longer period of time—even years (for example, when you are preparing for exams, or remembering traffic signals). This happens in a different way.

If the brain needs to transform short-term information into a long-term memory it begins by breaking it down into pieces, defined by categories. These categories include words, odours, colours, fruits and vegetables, numbers, etc. So, when you want to remember a diagram with labels, the brain would break it into colours, patterns and words. Remarkably, according to different categories, parts of the same information are stored in different storage areas of the brain. This entire operation of breaking down information according to the categories and storing it in different areas of the brain is performed by the *hippocampus*. When needed to recall memory, the brain is also able to rapidly recollect information from different parts and reassemble it.

The fact that the brain has different compartments for different kinds of memories explains why some individuals have a special ability for certain skills. For instance, mathematicians and scientists have a highly developed memory area for numbers and equations, and great designers have a more evolved area to store colors and patterns.[4]

Why do we remember certain things and forget others?

This is an interesting topic for neuroscientists and is still a developing area. Our current understanding is that there are two very important genes—*CREB Activator and CREB Repressor* which govern the formation of memories. The CREB activator stimulates the formation of long-term memory from the current short-term memory, while CREB Repressors then stop the same and eventually the short-term memory is forgotten. Now, what is the need of CREB Repressors? The answer is—the brain has a limited capacity in terms of memory and some memories need to be forgotten. For instance, imagine a scenario when one is reading a book for an examination and the doorbell rings. Two short-term memories are created; one is the text from the book and the other is the ringing of the doorbell. While the first needs to be retained with the help of the CREB Activator, the ringing of the door is of no significance for a long-term memory. Hence, the CREB Repressor will be released and the brain will soon forget the instance of door bell ringing.

This also explains why we remember some memories better than others. For instance, emotional memories are very strong—some tend to remain for life. This is because emotions tend to increase the CREB Activator gene and hence memories with strong emotional connections are immediately passed for long-term storage. This also explains why rote learning never works well—uninterested reading generates very little CREB Activator and in fact generates CREB Repressors, which makes one quickly forget things memorized without any logic.

Another aspect is that the CREB Activator is only limited and gets exhausted if used too much. Of course, they are regenerated within a short interval. That is why studying while taking short intervals in between is the best way to learn.

Does the brain burn calories too?

Actually, the brain burns a lot of calories! Although the average adult human brain weighs about 1.4 kilograms, which is only 2 per cent of the total body weight, it demands 20 per cent of our resting metabolic rate (RMR)—which is the total amount of energy our bodies expend in twenty-four hours if we do no work. RMR varies from person to person depending on age, gender, size and health but on an average it is about 1300 calories, or 60 per cent of the total calories burnt on an average day. This means that the brain consumes 260 calories just to keep things in order, roughly equal to the amount of calories burnt in running for 3 km. That's about 10.8 calories every hour. This translates to about 12.6 watts of power consumption every hour—enough to keep a small CFL lamp burning all day.

But given the functions which are performed, the human brain is way more energy efficient than any computer we have invented. For instance, IBM's Watson, the supercomputer that contests humans in intelligence, depends on ninety IBM Power and 750 servers, each of which requires around 1000 watts, that is, 7,50,000 watts in total.[5]

So can one burn calories by thinking hard?

It is unlikely that the calorie consumption of the brain varies much with the amount of thinking one does. Most of the brain is almost always occupied with the routine functions of breathing, involuntary muscular actions and other essential activities. Also, since the brain controls your state of hunger as well, any fatigue in the brain is accompanied with hunger. That is why one feels hungry after concentrating deeply on studies!

What is MRI?

One of the most important inventions in the field of neurology has been that of the MRI—Magnetic Resonance Imaging. It has helped us to decode the thinking of a human brain and get an insight into its functioning.

Radio waves are a type of an electromagnetic radiation which can pass through a human tissue without damaging it. MRI machines take advantage of this fact and allow the waves to freely penetrate through the skull, which helps the scientists to trace out the thoughts moving inside the brain.

Most of us have seen these MRI machines. We have watched them in movies and science-based series on television, where the patient is made to enter a huge cylindrical structure. They have a magnetic field which is twenty to sixty thousand times larger than the strength of the Earth's magnetic field.

This is how the MRI machines work: the patient lies flat and is made to enter the MRI machine. The machine is made up of two large coils which create the magnetic field. When this magnetic field is turned on, the nucleus of the atoms inside the body align horizontally in the direction of the field. A small pulse of energy is then passed through it which turns these nuclei upside down.

When the nuclei later revert to their original position, they emit a secondary pulse of radio energy which is analysed by the MRI machine. By analysing that, the MRI machine reconstructs a remarkable image of the inside of the brain. With the help of such images, computers then create for us beautiful diagrams of the brain in three dimensions.

MRI machines are less harmful than X-ray machines because they do not emit harmful ions. However, these machines are extremely costly and hence, the doctors need to share such facility. But just like technology, development will bring down the cost over time.

What is *grey matter* and how is it different from *white matter* in the brain?

The central nervous system in a human body can be divided into two parts—white matter and grey matter. They are so named because of the difference in their appearance. White matter appears white due to the presence of large amounts of *myelin*—a fatty protein that serves as an insulation function—which assists in signal transmission, whereas the grey matter appears grey-brown due to the presence of *neuronal cell bodies* and the relative lack of myelin. There is a difference in grey matter and white matter in terms of their components, functions as well as their contribution to the brain volume and energy consumption.

White matter connects the different areas of grey matter to the brain and the spinal cord. They carry nerve impulses from one neuron to another, thereby helping in faster transmission of nerve signals.

Grey matter mainly contains cell bodies, dendrites and synapses. In contrast to white matter, which mainly serves to transmit nerve signals, grey matter is where such signals are generated and processed. While white matter constitutes about 60 per cent of the brain volume, grey matter makes up the other 40 per cent. Grey matter, however, is more energy consuming and uses up approximately 94 per cent of the total oxygen that goes to the brain.

How is the right brain different from left brain?

One of the peculiar features of the human brain is that it is divided into two hemispheres—the left brain and the right brain. Neuroscientist Dr Roger W Sperry, California Institute of Technology, showed us that the two hemispheres of the brain are not identical to each other and are responsible for different functions in the body. He went on to receive a Nobel Prize for the same in 1981. This study by Dr Sperry brought about a great transformation in the field of neurology.

The right brain controls the left part of the body whereas the left brain controls the right part of the body. Hence, damage to one side of the brain affects the opposite side of the body.

The left brain processes the hearing and speech functions in the body. It carries out mathematical and logical computations and also controls language. It is mainly in charge of spatial abilities, face recognition and processing music. The right brain, on the other hand, helps to understand visual images and make sense of what we see.

One of the best examples to understand the difference between the right and the left brain is to note the difference in the manner in which people give directions. People with a dominant left brain will be very specific—'Take the first right from the fourth building on the street, go about 500 metres, take a left and then you reach the XYZ street' while on the other hand, the right brain will convey the directions like this—'Look at that red-coloured building, take a right from there. You will find a large blue-coloured school building at the end of the street from where you can take a left and you will reach the XYZ Street.'

To conclude, we can say that the left brain looks at the pieces first and then puts them together to get the whole picture whereas the right brain looks at the whole picture first and then the details.

So, if they are so different, how do they function together?

There is no right or wrong with respect to the left brain and the right brain; they are two different ways of thinking. Both parts of the brain coexist in harmony. Both the hemispheres communicate information with each other, such as sensory observations through the thick *corpus callosum.*

The left brain and the right brain process the information in a different manner. The left brain is verbal and analytical while the right brain is visual and artistic. Both the right and left brains work in a complementary manner and process the necessary information needed to provide the best results for the human being.

Let us understand the same with the help of a simple example. Imagine you are in a mathematics class and you are given various problems to solve as part of a project. However, you not only need to find the correct mathematical answers but also need to present them in a very creative manner in order to earn the best grades. So first of all, our analytical left brain will begin working out answers for all the problems which are asked to be solved. Once we have got the answers, our right brain will use its creativity and present these answers in the best possible manner. Thus, through coordination and joint efforts, the left and the right brains provide answers to various kinds of questions and situations in our life.

I am sure that larger animals, such as elephants and whales, have more neurons than human beings. Then why are they not more intelligent than us?

It is true that an elephant's brain has about three times the number of neurons compared to that of a human being.

However, 97.5 per cent of the neurons in the elephant brain (251 billion) are found in the cerebellum. In contrast, the elephant's cerebral cortex (outer layer of brain used for intelligence, calculations, decision and memory) holds only 5.6 billion neurons, about one-third of the number of neurons found in the human cerebral cortex. In fact, the human cerebral cortex has the largest number of neurons compared to any species. This high density of neurons in the cerebral cortex gives us the highest intelligence amongst all species. Here is a list of neurons in the cerebral cortex of different species.

SPECIES	NEURONS IN THE CEREBRAL CORTEX
Rat	40,00,000
Dog	16,00,00,000
Cat	30,00,00,000
Horse	1,20,00,00,000
Gorilla	4,30,00,00,000
Chimpanzee	5,50,00,00,000
Dolphin	5,80,00,00,000
Whale	10,50,00,00,000
Human	23,00,00,00,000

COUNT OF NEURONS IN THE CEREBRAL CORTEX

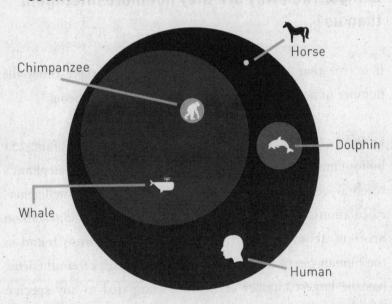

Notice that going by the count of neurons in the cerebral cortex, a human is twice as intelligent as a whale, a cat twice as smart as a dog, while chimpanzees are amongst the smartest monkeys.

How can I become a neuroscientist?

Neuroscience is a very wide field and depending on what specific aspect one wants to work with, it can cover dimensions of medical science, engineering and psychology.

From the medical angle, one can pursue a career as a neurosurgeon or even a neuro physician. This would involve treating people with neural disorders such as Alzheimer's or other forms of neuron loss, stroke, epilepsy or memory loss. Neurosurgery is considered to be one of the most difficult forms of surgeries, which requires a high level of expertise. With the rising number of victims in strokes and accident-related traumas, the next generation of neurosurgeons will be required to work extensively with computer-and robot-assisted surgery. Being a neurosurgeon is similar to any other medical profile. It would require science with biology at the 10 and 10+2 levels and then an MBBS or other such bachelor's programmes in medicine. After that one has to pursue a master's programme, such as Doctor of Medicine (DM) program (also called MD in some universities) for super specialization in neurology. One can also study further up to the PhD level in this field. Many leading Indian medical institutions including AIIMS (Delhi), SGPGIMS (Lucknow) and quite a few other government and private hospitals offer excellent programmes in neurology. One can also pursue a master's or a PhD programme abroad; UCLA (Los Angeles), John Hopkins University (Baltimore) and University of California (San Francisco) are considered amongst the best in the global arena.

But neuroscience is not just a domain of medicine and doctors. Unravelling the mysteries of the brain is also a subject of interest for an engineer but, of course, from a more application-based perspective. The challenge of enabling devices to be controlled directly by the brain, or the brain machine interface, and also using the working of the brain as a way to evolve the next generation of computing is an exciting future opportunity. We have seen electrical engineers and robotic experts working on such next-generation machines which are brain mapped, and in the next fifteen years we will probably see humanoids or robots which look like humans being completely controlled by the brains of their human masters. An engineer's route in neuroscience would require you to earn an engineering degree in electrical, electronics, mechanical or computer science at the bachelor's level. While doing your engineering you may like to develop projects which help you in understanding the specific areas of neuroscience-based engineering. To be successful, you will have to pursue a master's level or even a PhD. At this higher study level, you can choose many subjects related to artificial intelligence, robotics and electromagnetic analysis of the brain. It would be a good idea to keep exploring and remain updated with the new happenings in the field of neuroscience, and also write to some of the well-known professors and experts in the area to understand their perspectives and opportunities.

Another area of neuroscience relates not to the hardware but the software aspect of the brain—thoughts and their effects. This is the area of cognitive neuroscience— the study of human cognition or thought. This is the domain of a psychologist. Basically, the goal of this type of neuroscience is to understand how the physical and biological parts of the brain influence or create the less tangible parts, like thoughts, emotions, behaviours and memories. Such a career would need understanding and expertise in the field of psychology, especially applied psychology, which can be pursued with either humanities or science at 10+2 level.

 **MEET THE EXPERT:
JOGI V. PATTISAPU, MD FAAP FAANS**

Pediatric Neurosurgery
College of Medicine
University of Central Florida
Orlando FL

Q. Tell us what exactly you do.

Basically, paediatric neurosurgery involves dealing with the surgical disorders of a child's nervous system. In most cases we deal with issues that affect the development of a child's brain such as trauma, birth defects, brain tumours and conditions involving spinal fluid circulation (or hydrocephalus).

A paediatric neurosurgeon spends a good portion of time dealing with hydrocephalus, where too much spinal fluid under increased pressure affects the brain's ability to function properly. This condition is more common in developing countries and demands a significant amount of focused energy to handle this complex situation.

We attend to patients in the outpatient clinic and identify disorders that require surgical intervention. Surgery on the brain requires patience, dedication, hard work and many hours of focused attention to obtain the best results.

Q. When did you first decide to pursue a career in neurosurgery?

My first involvement with neurosurgery was in medical school (in my late leens), when I had the opportunity to witness operations on the brain. The overall excitement and thrill of seeing the brain and actually touching it and handling it was more than I could bear. My entire being was affected by this phenomenon of God's creation, which overwhelms everything else on this Earth.

This led me to pursue a career in this field and about fifteen years later I had the opportunity to become a paediatric neurosurgeon. Fortunately, I was blessed with a natural ability and many teachers guided me in my career. They offered me an opportunity to explore my talents in this field, and I used it to help many children and families.

Over the past several decades, it has been thrilling to follow the various developments in this wonderful field and to interact with the inquisitive and thrilling personalities who have shaped neurosurgery. In my own career I have come across many dedicated individuals who sacrificed much to find better ways of helping children and adults with devastating neurosurgical problems. I am truly indebted to them for their giving attitude and for having personally influenced my life in a positive way.

Q. You understand the human brain very well. Do you think we can ever build computers which match the human brain?

This is a very intriguing idea and I am eagerly waiting for young minds to find newer and more improved methods for such possibilities. But at this juncture, however, our knowledge and abilities are somewhat limited. Although we are able to recreate portions of the complex brain functions, we are still unable to understand and reproduce some of these higher cortical functions.

More specifically, we can assist people in regaining some aspects of hearing, sight and even some basic motor functions. Computers can help us with these functions and phenomenon. However, the ability to think and feel, to explore human emotions and understand human psychology is yet to be explored. In the future though, deep brain stimulation and focal control of brain functions will foster our ability to improve function, regain lost senses, use muscles more effectively and perhaps even change personalities. These advances will hopefully contribute in a more positive way to minimize suffering, and I look to the future generations to show us the way.

Such explorations will help patients overcome traumatic brain damage, congenital abnormalities (birth defects), degenerative conditions and complex disorders such as brain tumours, hydrocephalus, etc.

We are eagerly awaiting great advances in understanding brain physiology and our ability to influence its functions by the next generation who are sure to find more answers for these complex questions.

Q. **What do you think are the most important qualities for a successful neuroscientist?**

Basically most qualities that make anyone successful are necessary to be a successful neuroscientist.

As with any endeavour, hard work, dedication, concentration and focus are most important. This only comes with constant studying and avoidance of distractions. Young people today have far more distractions than ever due to technological advances and increased exposure to the media. Unfortunately, very few of these offer good role models for the next generation. We must keep looking for idealists to emulate. Keeping such ideals in front of us allows one to remain focused on the path for obtaining delayed gratification.

Read good books routinely and rely on your teachers for guidance. We need to dream big and have a great vision if we want to reach great heights to tackle the complex problems in neurosciences. I only wish the youth of today remains on the right path for a bit longer and works a bit harder to reach higher ideals. I believe anything is possible, and great leaders and good thinkers are daily reminders for us.

Please remember, we may be able to reach Mars or the Moon, but conquering our own mind requires as much if not more concentration and hard work.

I wish you all the very best in your studies.

 ## NOTE TO PARENTS

Neuroscience is a very challenging and exciting career, with the increasing understanding of the human brain and the ailments which affect the brain—both medical and non-medical perspectives. Neurosurgeons and neuro physicians are in demand by hospitals and research institutions across the world. New drugs for treating neurons are being constantly researched by pharmaceutical companies across the world.

Neuroscience, in all forms, is a very rewarding career, with numerous opportunities to make new discoveries as it is still an area which has not been completely explored. But becoming a neuroscientist is a long academic process and only a few universities offer advanced courses in the field.

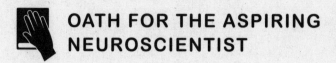

OATH FOR THE ASPIRING NEUROSCIENTIST

'I will be remembered for creating a new understanding of the human brain and thereby helping the scientific community understand how memories, thoughts and decisions are processes, which may also enable the medical community to treat neural disorders.'

(Write this oath in the space below. You can also add new thoughts and goals for yourself as a neuroscientist.)

_____

_____

_____

_____

_____

1   Brain Facts and Figures. https://faculty.washington.edu/chudler/facts.html
2   http://io9.com/5890414/the-4-biggest-myths-about-the-human-brain
3   http://hassans.de/sami/?p=79
4   Michio Kaku, *The Future of the Mind*
5   http://www.scientificamerican.com/article/thinking-hard-calories/

CHAPTER 6

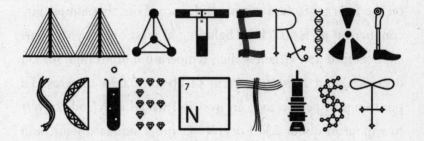

On 7 May 2014, Srijan and I were scheduled to leave Delhi for London at 10.30 a.m. on a British Airways flight. However, there was an email and an SMS early in the morning stating that our flight had been delayed by four hours. When we called up the airline office, they informed us that the delay was due to a technical error with the aircraft. The aircraft we were supposed to be travelling in was a *Boeing 777 ER*, the largest twin engine aircraft ever built. Such an aircraft would rarely function below expected standards. The report of a technical fault in this massive aircraft made both of us slightly concerned and highly curious.

While boarding the delayed flight, the captain came out to greet me. I immediately asked him, 'What had gone wrong?' Srijan added, 'What stalled one of the largest aircraft in the world?' The captain smiled and replied, 'Sir, the flight was delayed because we had to run a check-up of the aircraft after it was struck by lightning last night.' We were now curious to know more about the effect of lightning and the protection modern aircraft have against it.

Upon landing, we promptly opened our laptops and searched on the Internet to find out more. It turned out that almost any commercial jet is struck by lightning at least once a year. This exposes it to an extremely high temperature of around 30,000 degrees C and a strong current of up to 32,000 amperes. To put things in perspective: an iron rod would melt and convert to vapour at about 2300 degrees C and a standard light bulb consumes about a quarter of an ampere of current. Imagine how strong a single stroke of lightning is!

Even so, there has been no major aviation incident due to lightning for almost half a century now. I wondered what kind of technology was being deployed to keep passengers safe in such extreme situations. And how does the body of the plane, which is criss-crossed with multiple communication and electronic wiring, withstand such massive surges of charge and heat? What about the highly combustible fuel that it carries?

The answer is in the true convergence of material science, electrical engineering and physics. Read on to know more!

Planes are usually made of aluminium alloys which are excellent conductors of electricity. These alloys are used to form a metal sheet around the aircraft which, working on the concept called a 'Faraday cage', ensuring that lightning travels along the surface of the aircraft without entering the fuselage or the main body, keeping everyone safe inside. Even when planes are constructed from advanced composite materials, which are imperfect conductors, there is a special layer of conductive screen to carry the lightning current away from the plane.

This is how the convergence of science and technology is able to safeguard every single aircraft 30,000 feet up in the air from one of the most powerful processes of nature. This is how it affects and protects our lives every day.

● ● ●

Our journey in understanding the best of material science took a new turn when we visited Harvard University in 2011. There at the Harvard School for Engineering and Science we met Professor Vinothan Manoharan, who exemplifies the convergence of science in himself. He is a professor of chemical engineering and physics, and he showed us his work in bionanoscience. Professor Manoharan explained to us his latest work on biomaterials, which he calls self-assembling materials. As you know, DNA, the basic blocks of life particles, are like two strands held together with weak hydrogen bonds. This structure is also called the double helix. Although it may look complicated, the DNA in a cell is really just a pattern made up of four different smaller units of nucleotides called A, C, G and T respectively. These nucleotides are very specific in bonding with each other; for instance, typically A bonds with T, and C with G. When we met Professor Manoharan, he looked at his large computer screen and said, 'We will use this specific bonding to do something extraordinary for nanomaterials.' He and his group of three overseas PhD students took us to their lab where they showed us a small jar which seemed to hold plain water. As we looked at it, Professor Manoharan put in, 'Dr Kalam! This jar also contains water-soluble nanoparticles. I have treated them with biological DNA.'

Srijan asked, 'How large are these particles? Are they the size of atoms?'

'No,' replied Professor Manoharan. 'They are about the size of 300 or so atoms.'

'That is still nano-sized,' I said. A nano-sized object is the range of a few nanometres. Do you know what a nanometre is? It is 10^{-6} of a millimetre, that is, one-millionth of a millimetre. Nano-sized particles are materials with their length, breadth and height dimensions within the size range of 1 to 100 nanometres.

Professor Manoharan then explained the concept to us. 'Each of these particles is coated with about thirty layers of different DNA patterns. Each particle has its own unique and predetermined coating.' Then he pressed the Enter key on his computer and announced, 'I have now started their interaction with one another. When a particular type of DNA is applied on a particle at the atomic level, we are able to generate a prefixed behaviour and automatic assembly from them.'

Remember, DNA bonds only along certain ways. So these chemical particles which are covered with layers of DNA will interact and bond with each other in a way governed by the pattern of these coatings. First the outermost layers of coating interact and form a certain bond. Once this coating has done its job, the next inner layer of coating emerges and again a particular type of bonding happens. In a way, it is a bio-programming of atom level particles.

While right now this is effective only up to thirty layers of DNA coating, one on top of another, imagine the possibilities when this coating happens across millions of such layers in the future! It would be possible to just 'throw' billions of dust-like particles into space, who will know exactly how to interact with each other. They would build spaceships on their own, travel to planets, etc. They would then disintegrate only to start reassembling again to perhaps form a colony on different planets, all ready for humans to move in. This is the future of material science—as a result of the convergence of bioscience and chemistry.

Welcome to the world of material science. As you would expect, material science relies heavily on chemistry and an understanding of the properties of elements and compounds. But in the true sense, it is an interdisciplinary field which deals with the study of matter and its properties. It may also involve the discovery and design of new materials such as carbon composites. Basically it deals with matter from different perspectives—how to make them, what is their structure, what are their properties and performance standards.

Humanity's earliest stint with material science began with the engineering and processing of the most important material for survival. Can you guess what that material was? It was food!

About 4,00,000 years ago humans, who were merely hunters, had a new tool at their disposal—fire. With the discovery of fire, the caveman embarked on the earliest experiments in material science—the art of cooking food, which is technically heat processing of organic compounds. The next material which humans were exposed to was metal. The first metal to be used was gold, about 8000 years ago. Why gold? Well, that is primarily because gold naturally occurs in a very pure form. About 6000 years ago we learned to use copper and silver. These were perhaps the first to be used to make tools, weapons and utensils. Real material transformation of materials began when humans learned the process of alloying metals—combining one metal with another to get metal of more improved quality. The first alloy was bronze—a mixture of arsenic and copper and later of tin and copper. This happened about 5000 years ago.

Bronze proved to be harder and more durable than copper and quickly replaced it as the main component of weapons, building materials, armour and tools. In fact the period from 3000 BCE to about 1000 BCE is called the Bronze Age in human history. It is the period when the Indus Valley Civilization flourished. Then came the Iron Age, when humans learned to alloy iron—this time with carbon. Do you know pure iron is soft and hardly of any use? Humans learned that when you mix it with carbon, it becomes harder and stronger. For the next 2000 years iron remained the principal metal for manufacturing tools. A leap forward was made much later, when the English material scientist, Henry Bessemer discovered steel around 1855.

Today material science is a truly diverse field. It incorporates almost everything that we touch and see in our daily life. Material scientists make the material which help planes fly; they produce materials which glow on your monitors and screens; they make plastics, fuels, threads, medicinal materials, glues, inks, new strong metals, fireproof glassware in your kitchen and many, many more such useful things.

The Future of Material Science

The twenty-first century will see two trends in material science. First, there will be a focus on materials that are perfect in their properties, such as super-strong metals, perfect insulators or perfect conductors. This will be achieved by the nanosciences. Second, there will be a focus on creating materials which are specifically engineered for a very well-defined application— these require a specific density, conductivity, etc. With these two aspects in mind, we envision a multidimensional progress in the material sciences, such as:

1. **Bio-inspired materials:** Humankind has always been inspired by nature and the new-age materials will continue to derive their inspiration from nature. This is already happening in many fields. For instance, a Japanese company called Spiber is working on making artificial spiderweb, which is one of the strongest materials we know. The company has already managed to decode the genes responsible for the production of the protein fibroin, which spiders use to make their web. Spiber has in fact created bioengineered, or genetically-modified bacteria which can produce fibroin themselves. These bacteria are fed with sugar and salt, and, as a result of digestion, they create fibroin. It is estimated that a single gram of fibroin can make a 10 kilometre-long spiderweb or spider silk. Spiber predicts that mass-produced fibroin can be used to make auto parts, surgical materials and bulletproof vests. With such discoveries, Spiderman may soon be a reality!

Material scientists are also closely studying houseflies. If you observe them carefully, you will notice that their wings are light, thin and flexible enough to allow flight and yet strong enough to protect their soft bodies. This excited the researchers at Harvard University's Wyss Institute for Biologically Inspired Engineering, who have developed a new material called Shrilk. Shrilk replicates an insect cuticle's strength, durability and versatility. Shrilk is so called because it is composed of chitin, commonly extracted from discarded shrimp shells, and fibroin protein obtained from silk. This material can be used to make trash bags, packaging materials and diapers that degrade quickly and are yet strong enough to bear loads.

2. **Outer space applications:** In another forty years, humans will definitely start colonizing other planets. We estimate that by 2060, we will have permanent settlements on the Moon and Mars and by 2070, humans will be able to set up a civilization on Titan, the water-bearing moon of Saturn. All these bodies, as you know, have very different climatic conditions compared to Earth. For instance, the Moon has hardly any atmosphere; it has only one hundred trillionth of that of the Earth and mostly contains the element argon. The air on Mars, on the other hand, mostly consists of carbon dioxide—similar to the conditions that existed on Earth billions of years ago, before the Great Oxygenation Event (see the *Pathologist* chapter for details). Titan, one of the sixty-odd Moons of the planet Saturn, has an atmosphere rich in nitrogen and methane. It is also believed that it may have earth-like features like rain and winds, rivers, lakes and seas. But what rains there is not water, but liquid methane.

All these bodies have different gravities and temperatures compared to the Earth. Under normal circumstances, no life form, barring a few bacteria, would be able to live on any of these planets/moons. The next generation of material scientists will have to develop composite matter which can adapt to these unfriendly conditions. As a material scientist for space applications, you will have to completely re-engineer everything available on this planet—including developing new sources of oxygen and water, new fuels, and new building material to survive higher and lower gravities and huge storms. Perhaps, the research of Professor Vinod Manoharan might be instrumental in making this happen. Nanorobots could be sent decades in advance to planets we believe to be favourable for inhabiting. They may work on their own for years, transforming the planet, building settlements, air conditioning, generating water and finally making the soil capable of growing food. Once their work is complete, the first batch of settlers can be sent to start our own beyond-Earth settlements.

3. **New fuels and energy-efficient materials:** Another important future material science challenge will be to develop better fuel materials, better devices to store energy and also to reduce the carbon footprint generated by such fuels or storage devices. This would involve developing green sources of energy, such as those from bio-sources like jatropha, algae, etc. Material research is also looking at hydrogen fuel cells to power vehicles so that all they emit is warm water. Imagine how effectively this will check the ever-increasing threat of pollution from cars

and buses! This is already becoming a reality; we have travelled on a hydrogen-powered bus in Iceland. The only challenge remains in how to make this cheap enough to substitute regular fossil fuels. This may be achieved in the next ten years, by developing ultra-thin platinum coating, which will only be as thick as two atoms piled on top of each other and this is expected to significantly reduce the cost of the fuel cells.

4. **Nanomaterials:** One of the most promising branches in material science is that of developing nanomaterials and nanoengineering. Nanorobots will soon be able to go inside any material and test its quality and detect even minute faults within it. One prominently discussed nanomaterial is Carbon Nano-Tube or CNT. These are cylindrical forms of carbon material, with their lengths being up to 132 million times their thickness, significantly more than any other known substance. To put things in perspective, the drinking straw we commonly use at homes and restaurants is about 2 millimetres thick. Now imagine if this was made of CNT: its length would then be around 264 kilometres. So, essentially, sitting in Delhi, you could drink a glass of juice from Jaipur!

CNT is the strongest and toughest material invented till date. To get an idea of its strength, just imagine you have a long wire of CNT which is 1 millimetre in width and breadth. Such a wire will have the thickness of about four to five strands of human hair. Can you guess how much weight such a thin wire of CNT can support? 6422 kilograms! That means you can lift two full-grown elephants with this thin CNT wire. This makes it about eighteen times stronger than a diamond, about twenty times stronger than steel, about 200 times stronger than iron and roughly 500 times stronger than any human bone!

Now, if you have you seen the famous movie *X-Men*, you might remember the character Wolverine. With long blades coming out of the back of his hands, he can cut through wood, iron and practically any material around him. While this is in the realm of fiction, the reality is that in the near future we may see such blades made of CNT, which will be so sharp, thin and strong that they can act as a nanoknife, slicing through all standard materials by only using the power a human being can generate from his hands.

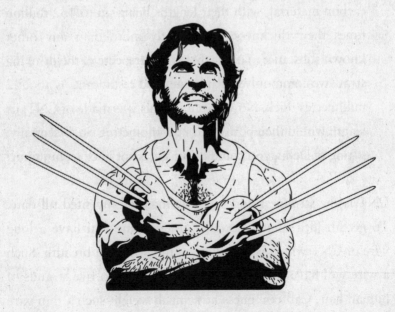

Besides this, CNT has another unique property in its thermal conductivity. While along its length it is ten times more heat conductive than copper, along its width its thermal conductivity is lower than that of normal soil. This property is called 'ballistic conduction' in the language of material science. All these properties make CNT an excellent material for machine parts, vehicles and even surgical tools. Such nanomaterials are indeed a futuristic application for material scientist—and we have to work towards making such material to suit outer space explorations.

CONVERSATIONS WITH A SCIENCE TEACHER

What makes different materials exhibit different properties and what differentiates them?

Atoms are the building blocks of all materials, no matter how simple or complex the material is. An element is composed of only one type of atom. For example, a lump of copper is made up of only copper atoms. Now, whenever atoms from two or more different elements combine together to form a molecule, we get a compound; for example, water is made up of two hydrogen atoms and one oxygen atom.

There are about 118 different types of atoms. This is because there are 118 different elements.

As you may have learned in school, compounds can be classified according to the type of bonding between their atoms and molecules. There are four major kinds of bonding in solids: covalent bonding, ionic bonding, metallic bonding and weak intermolecular bonding.

There are, however, an almost uncountable number of ways of combining atoms of different elements together. That is why there are almost an infinite number of different compounds.

Think about the number of different words we can make from just the twenty-six letters of the English alphabet. This will give you some idea of the number of different compounds that can be created from different arrangements of all the different atoms. Now since these compounds are made from different constituent elements, and with their atoms bonded in different ways, they exhibit varying ranges of properties such as density, conduction, ductility (ability to be drawn into a wire), malleability (ability to be beaten into thin sheets), radiation, etc.

How did humankind discover all these diverse elements and matter? Which was the first

element to be synthesized by a chemical process?

As one would expect, the discovery of different elements and other matter such as compounds and alloys occurred over long periods of human history. Some of the earliest metals and materials were simply 'picked up' by cavemen and hunters because they found them useful in the making of tools. This is how gold, copper, silver, chromium, zinc, tin, carbon and sulphur were discovered.

Rarer and generally more unstable forms of matter were discovered in a much more complicated manner. The earliest such chemical discovery was that of phosphorus by the German chemist Hennig Brand in 1669. He initially set out to discover the philosopher's stone, a mythical material which medieval people believed could turn lead into gold (it is called 'paaras' in Indian culture). Of course, today we know that there is no such thing, but back in those days chemists (or alchemists) would spend their entire lifetimes researching this. Hennig Brand was one such chemist. He exhausted all his money and time trying to make the philosopher's stone, but to no avail. Frustrated, he started conducting random experiments with practically anything which came to his mind. He kept on doing these stray experiments for years, until people began thinking he was insane.

Then around 1669 he had an idea. He heated human urine samples in a furnace until the retort or the glass container being used became red hot. He noticed that all of a sudden glowing fumes filled the retort and a liquid dripped out, bursting into flames. He could catch the liquid in a jar and cover it, where it solidified and continued to give off a pale-green glow. What he collected was phosphorus, which he named from the Greek word meaning 'light-bearing' or 'light-bearer'. This is how the first human extraction of an element truly came from a waste product! Brand was not that excited about his discovery, because he kept trying to use this phosphorus to produce gold from lead—enterprise which was of course never successful. For him his discovery of phosphorus was a failure. Also, his process was extremely inefficient as it produced just 150 grams of phosphorus after procuring and processing 6000 litres of human urine!

This experiment started a chain reaction and material scientists kept searching for newer and newer elements of matter. With the philosopher's stone finally proven to be a fable, scientists around the 1750s became more interested in first understanding the properties of the elements found. Incidentally, the lightest and the most abundant element in the universe, hydrogen, was discovered only in 1766 by the British material scientist Henry Cavendish. More interestingly, it was only about 200 years ago, in 1771, that the life-giving oxygen was discovered by the Swedish chemist Carl Wilhelm Scheele.

The most remarkable work in the direction of finding new materials was done by the Russian scientist Dmitri Mendeleev. In

1863, scientists knew only of fifty-six different elements (today we can identify 118). As a chemistry teacher, Mendeleev was always keen to find out what constituted the chemical properties of matter and their patterns. He kept thinking about it for days. It is said that he envisioned the answers to the problem in a dream, when he saw a table with rows and columns, along which different elements were lined up. He later recounted:

'I saw in a dream a table where all the elements fell into place as required. Awakening, I immediately wrote it down on a piece of paper. Only in one place did a correction later seem necessary.'

Mendeleev produced his work and made a presentation to the Royal Chemical Society where for the first time someone classified elements according to their atomic weight and valence. Elements could be arranged according to their increasing atomic weight, in a table—called the Periodic Table. He proved that if such an arrangement is done, elements across a column display similar properties such as strength, chemical reactions, conductivity and sometimes even the way they look. He then boldly stated that in the near future people must prepare for the discovery of new elements similar to aluminum and silicon, whose properties he predicted even before they were formally discovered. An admirer of Indian science and Sanskrit, he chose to call these elements Eka-aluminium and Eka-silicon (eka means one in Sanskrit). People mocked him for making such predictions, but when in 1875, Gallium (Eka-aluminium) and in 1886, Germanium (Eka-silicon) were discovered Mendeleev was indeed proved correct. Largely owing to the forecasts of Mendeleev, scientists all around the world were inspired to search for the predicted elements missing from the table. Between 1875 and 1900, twenty new elements were discovered.

```
                     Ti = 50    Zr = 90    ? = 180.
                     V = 51     Nb = 94    Ta = 182.
                     Cr = 52    Mo = 96    W = 186.
                     Mn = 55    Rh = 104,4  Pt = 197,4.
                     Fe = 56    Rn = 104,4  Ir = 198.
               Ni = Co = 59     Pl = 106,8  O = 199.
    H = 1             Cu = 63,4  Ag = 108   Hg = 200.
         Be = 9,4 Mg = 24 Zn = 65,2  Cd = 112
         B = 11   Al = 27,4 ? = 68   Ur = 116  Au = 197?
         C = 12   Si = 28   ? = 70   Sn = 118
         N = 14   P = 31   As = 75   Sb = 122  Bi = 210?
         O = 16   S = 32   Se = 79,4 Te = 128?
         F = 19   Cl = 35,5 Br = 80  I = 127
    Li = 7 Na = 23  K = 39  Rb = 85,4 Cs = 133  Tl = 204.
                     Ca = 40 Sr = 87,6 Ba = 137  Pb = 207.
                     ? = 45  Ce = 92
                     ?Er = 56 La = 94
                     ?Yt = 60 Di = 95
                     ?In = 75,6 Th = 118?
```

Who discovered radioactive elements?

Radioactive materials are composed of atoms which are unstable and end up losing energy by emitting radiations in the form of alpha (2 protons + 2 neutrons), beta (electrons) or gamma (only electromagnetic) radiations. This property is called radioactivity.

Radioactivity was first discovered by the French scientist Henri Becquerel in 1896 after an experiment with 'glowing' particles in a cathode ray tube (earlier used in televisions). But no single person can be entirely credited with its discovery; in fact the responsibility should be shared among the four legends of chemistry and physics, who were contemporaries: Ernest Rutherford of Britain. Pierre Curie and his wife, Marie Curie of France and Frederick Soddy, his brilliant student.

The most outstanding among these earliest nuclear scientists was Marie Curie, who discovered polonium and radium and evolved the theory of radioactivity. Her life is a story of great achievement, which unfortunately came to a tragic end. She was the first woman to win the Nobel Prize, the only woman to receive the award in two fields, and the only person ever to win in multiple sciences, namely physics (1903) and chemistry (1911).

Today, we know that radioactive elements are lethal for the human body, leading to cancer and other fatal illnesses. That is why doctors are so careful when they conduct X-rays on you— to keep the exposure minimum. But in the early 1900s, material scientists were not aware of this. In fact, Marie Curie used to carry radioactive elements in test tubes in her pockets, which would glow when left in darkness. Eventually, those radioactive elements, the very ones she discovered, poisoned her body with their radiation. She died from aplastic anaemia in 1934, a common disease occurring due to uncontrolled exposure to radiation. Today, the souvenirs from her life—her notebook, her cookbook and pens—are stored in lead containers to protect viewers from the lethal radiation they still emit.

Is there a possibility that there are still some forms of matter we have not discovered yet?

Absolutely! Most of the stable elements have already been discovered thanks to the predictive work of Mendeleev. However, many new elements can still be found but they will have higher atomic weight as all lighter elements have already been discovered. This also means they will be very unstable and hence highly radioactive and so will rapidly decay into smaller elements. In all likelihood they will only be man-made and have short survival periods. Even then, they will be highly unstable and last for only a few milliseconds, and in this short time you will have to isolate and preserve them.

Since 1980, about twelve new elements have been discovered; all of them are highly radioactive. The latest element to be discovered is called ununseptium. It is the heaviest chemical element to be ever found. Its temporary symbol is 'Uus', its atomic number is 117 and it has an atomic weight of 294. It was discovered by a joint research team of American and Russian material scientists. Ununseptium, which literally means one hundred and seventeen, is so heavy that if you fill its liquid form in a standard two-litre bottle, the bottle will weigh over 32 kilos, more than the weight of a filled cooking gas cylinder.

Why is diamond considered the hardest substance on Earth? What makes it so hard?

Diamond is not the hardest substance, but only the hardest naturally occurring mineral we are aware of. As you know, diamonds are the crystallized form of carbon created under extreme heat and pressure. It's this process that makes diamonds so hard.

If you look at the molecular structure of diamonds you'd notice that they are made of carbon atoms linked together in a lattice structure, almost like a thick mesh. Each carbon atom in this mesh shares electrons with four other carbon atoms forming a tetrahedral unit. This tetrahedral bonding of five carbon atoms forms an incredibly strong molecule, which lends strength to diamonds.

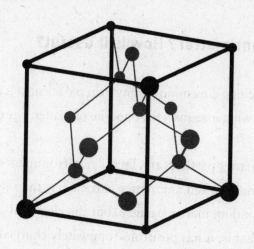

Man has always tried to manufacture diamonds artificially. In 1951, General Electric (GE) launched Project Super-pressure, where an attempt was made to create diamonds from graphite by applying massive amounts of pressure and heat in machines called diamond presses. The project failed to produce a single diamond no matter how much pressure was applied.

Then material scientists tried to find diamonds inside a crater in Arizona which had been formed by a meteorite that crashed into the Earth. In addition to its size and heat, the meteorite had one other significant component. It contained metal. So scientists reasoned, what if they could make diamonds by generating a small-scale meteorite crash in a laboratory? They combined carbon atoms with the liquid metal troilite and added excessive heat and pressure. Can you guess the result of this experiment? Solid diamonds!

What is antimatter? How is it useful?

The next exciting dimension for any material scientist is antimatter. It is exactly what it seems—the opposite of matter. Let us explain.

These antimatter particles are, literally, mirror images of normal matter particles. Each antimatter particle has the same mass as its corresponding matter particle, but the electrical charges are opposite, that is, it has positrons (oppositely charged electrons) and antiprotons (oppositely charged protons).

You might have heard that matter cannot be created or destroyed, but modern material scientists and physicists have proved this theory wrong. Einstein showed that matter can not only be destroyed but also be converted to energy. In fact, according to Einstein's mass-energy equation ($E=mc^2$), the single feather of a bird, if destroyed, would produce enough energy to boil 160 million litres of water! Now how can matter be destroyed? When antimatter comes into contact with normal matter, these equal but opposite particles collide to produce an explosion emitting pure radiation, which travels out of the point of the explosion at the speed of light. Both particles that created the explosion are completely annihilated.

Many modern scientific theories tell us that the Big Bang was nothing but the collision of a large number of matter and antimatter particles.

I have seen antimatter guns in some science fiction movies. Is it actually possible to make such a weapon?

Theoretically, the existence of antimatter particles opens up the possibility of harnessing immense energy from the very source which gave birth to the universe. In fact, approximately 10 grams of antiprotons would be enough fuel to allow a manned spacecraft to reach Mars in only a month. Today, it takes nearly a year for an unmanned spacecraft to reach Mars. Unfortunately, just like with any source of energy, the same vast energy can also be used as a weapon, such as an antimatter gun.

The problem with extracting energy from antimatter is twofold. First, there is almost no antimatter left in the universe; probably all of it was consumed during the Big Bang and the creation of the universe. Second, even if antimatter is artificially created, it would be extremely difficult to store it in any container, because it would destroy the container made out of matter. The latest work in the field of storing antimatter revolves around storing it in a vacuum tube with a magnetic field to hold it in place. But it is still a long way off from being a stable storage element.

What is the most expensive element?

The most expensive natural element is called francium. Although francium occurs naturally, it decays so quickly that it cannot be collected for use. Only a few atoms of francium have been produced commercially so far. If you want to produce 100 grams of francium, you could expect to pay a few billion US dollars for it. Hence, there are no sellers of francium right now. Lutetium is the most expensive element that you can actually order. The price for 100 grams of lutetium is around $10,000 (approximately Rs 5.5 lakh).

The transuranium (heavier than uranium) elements, in general, are extremely expensive. These elements typically are man-made, and it is costly to isolate them from impurities. For example, californium is estimated to cost around $2.7 billion dollars per 100 grams. So, if our entire nation pooled in its annual wealth, we would be able buy only about 6 kilos of this material! You can contrast that price with the cost of plutonium, which runs between $5000 and $13,000 for 100 grams (Rs 3 to 8 lakh), depending on purity.

How can I be a great material scientist?

Material science is all about the convergence of different subjects. As a material scientist, you may invent new computer chips or artificial bones or spacecraft material or nano-level insulators or even better super glue. The possibilities and opportunities are endless. Hence, while choosing to become a material scientist, it would also be useful to spend some time thinking about what category of material you would like to discover and work on. We would suggest that you pick from categories of biological applications, nano-applications, energy and fuels, space-based materials and electronics, as they will be the greatest transformational technologies of the future. Depending on this choice, you will have to orient your studies and readings from now onwards.

Almost compulsorily, you will have to be among the best in chemistry; developing materials begins with understanding chemicals and their properties. Physics and mathematics are also important. Physics will explain to you the properties of matter and mathematics is necessary for solving complex functions, which a material scientist has to deal with.

Most of the next-generation experiments in materials are first run as computer simulations, hence understanding computer programming is an added bonus.

A great material scientist has oodles of curiosity, perseverance and focus. You should develop a questioning mind, constantly seeking knowledge. Make a special material scientist diary. When you start working in laboratories, you should ask your teachers about the chemicals you see there and take notes. When you come across an interesting article on a new development in the field, note it down in your diary. Reflect on how the latest trend is moving in the world of material science.

After your 10+2 with science, you will have many options to consider. Many of the IITs and other good institutions offer great courses at the bachelor's as well as master's level in chemical and metallurgical fields. There are also many specific laboratories run by the Council of Scientific and Industrial Research (CSIR) which deal with specific materials such as:

- AMPRI (Advanced Materials and Processes Research Institute, Bhopal)
- CBRI (Central Building Research Institute, Roorkee)
- CGCRI (Central Glass and Ceramic Research Institute, Kolkata)
- NML (National Metallurgical Laboratory, Jamshedpur)

- NCL (National Chemical Laboratory, Pune)
- IMMT (Institute of Minerals and Materials Technology, Bhubaneswar)
- IIP (Indian Institute of Petroleum, Dehradun)

All these institutions are funded by the government and they promote new applied research in their respective fields. To join them, you will have to complete your master's degree.

There are some great international courses in material science. Most of the well-known institutions offer this area of study, like Massachusetts Institute of Technology (MIT), Harvard University, Stanford University, which are all in the United States, Tohoku University in Japan, ETH Zurich in Switzerland and Nanyang Technological University in Singapore.

As a great material scientist you should think big—target a Nobel Prize in chemistry or physics!

 # MEET THE EXPERT: DR A.P.J. ABDUL KALAM

Q. It is said that one of the happiest moments of your professional career was while working with new materials. Can you tell us more about it?

I have spent a large part of my scientific career developing materials which can be used in missiles, rockets and other defence applications. These materials have to be high on strength, heat resistant and yet lightweight. I had a unique experience during one such material development which left a lasting impression on me.

This happened during the 1990s when we were developing the material needed for the Agni missile. No nation was willing to help us, even with a screw, so every single part of this landmark missile system had to be indigenously produced. Of course, this was a difficult task but we were determined to give India its best missile system. One of the materials we were developing was a carbon-carbon composite, which could be used for missile nose shields as it is lightweight and heat resistant.

Around this time, I happened to visit a hospital in Hyderabad. There I found many children struggling to walk with artificial calipers (limbs) weighing over 4 kilos. The weight of these limbs was slowing them down and making movement very strenuous.

At the request of Professor B.N. Prasad, head of the orthopaedic department at the Nizam's Institute of Medical Sciences, I asked my friends working on Agni if it was possible to use the composite material we had created for Agni's heat shield to make artificial limbs for polio-affected patients. They agreed it could be.

The project immediately caught our attention and interest. We worked on this for some time and came up with a prosthesis (the technical term for this is 'floor reaction orthosis') that weighed around 400 grams, thus reducing the weight the child was carrying by 90 per cent.

With the help of the doctors at the institute, we fitted the new, lightweight limbs on the children who could now easily walk and run around. Everyone was ecstatic! Parents who were present at the time shed tears of joy on seeing their children moving easily with the help of the light calipers. With the lightweight device provided by the hospital they could run, ride a bicycle and do all sorts of things they had been deprived of for a long time. This experiment in material science was a grand success.

The freedom attained by the children gave me a great joy, which I never experienced during any other achievement in my life. Of course, later the same material was used to shield the Agni missile system and thus a double benefit was reaped from the new material we had developed.

NOTE TO PARENTS

Material science is definitely a great career of the future which is more research oriented than any other technological career. We have met numerous successful material science entrepreneur-scientists both in India and abroad such solar cells, superconductors, new types of coatings and paints, biomaterials and many more. The 2014 Nobel Prize for Physics was awarded to three scientists, Isamu Akasaki, Hiroshi Amano and Shuji Nakamura who invented a new semiconductor material, the blue light-emitting diode.

In the times ahead, we envision tremendous demand for material scientists, right from toothpaste manufacturing units to spaceship building enterprises. Convergence of science will enable complex applications of material science such as self-assembling particles and artificial human organs; innovative researchers will be needed in these domains. New fuels will have to be discovered, and we believe that existing energy companies will deploy material scientists which can enable them to move to newer sources of energy—biofuels and efficient solar panels.

For a truly successful career in this field one must pursue education to a very high level; a PhD is almost a must in this domain. Most PhD programmes in India and abroad are fully scholarship based or offer stipends and tuition fee waivers to students.

If your child aspires to be a material scientist, you should encourage him or her to read about nanoengineering, radioactivity and about how materials for structures like buildings, aircraft and ships are manufactured.

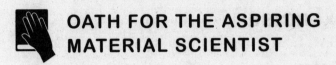

OATH FOR THE ASPIRING MATERIAL SCIENTIST

'As a great material scientist, I will be remembered for developing new materials which can enable humans to inhabit other planets and also create new fuels which can help save and preserve our planet itself.'

(Write this oath in the space below. You can also add new thoughts and goals for yourself as a material scientist.)

_____

_____

_____

_____

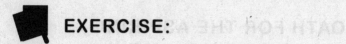

EXERCISE:

The year is 2050.

The human population has increased to the 12 billion people. Asia alone now has over 7 billion people living in it. The world has realized it is critical now to find a new planet to live in.

You are the head of a new division under the United Nations to explore new planets for settlements. This is called the **INTER**planet **ST**rike for **EL**evating **A**lternative **R**egions, popularly called INTERSTELLAR, named after a movie made on this topic about forty years ago on a similar theme.

INTERSTELLAR has been given a list of two likely planets located far off but still within a five-year travel period from our planet in nearby solar systems. Considering how large the universe is, this is just a stone's throw away!

Two probes have already been sent to these planets and the reports are promising. The gravity and heat are suitable for human habitation and the world is excited about the possibilities.

However, as head of INTERSTELLAR you know that there will be significant problems. Humans are very sensitive to the environment and need a certain suitable mix of gases and water to survive. Moreover, the crust of the planet needs to bear soil in order for plants to grow, and hence produce necessary food.

Thankfully, you have the World Nanotech University (WNU) in New Delhi for help. They have promised to design nanorobots which can be sent to any planet in order to conduct the necessary chemical reactions to produce any necessary compounds such as oxygen or water. However, you need to programme them for a particular reaction.

1. Planet 1, called Zioux, faces a serious challenge—water. There is barely 1 per cent water on it, and your INTERSTELLAR team tells you that we need at least 30 per cent water to survive on it. Probes have, however, shown one interesting finding. The planet is filled with calcium hydroxide, a white powder spread all over its surface. You are wondering if this can be converted into water. WNU's robots are capable of carrying gas packets to start any reaction. INTERSTELLAR needs you to determine what gas they should carry to make the necessary water from the available calcium hydroxide powder. Can you quickly find this out and give the necessary instructions?

2. The second planet is called Femto, and it contains water in abundance but lacks a critical component—oxygen. It is also quite cold, with temperatures less than -10 degrees C. Initially, INTERSTELLAR thought they would electrolyze the water into oxygen but that proved to be a costly process in terms

of energy, especially in the cold weather, and so the plan was disbanded. Then the latest probe highlighted something which excited everyone. The planet is filled with sodium chlorate. INTERSTELLAR wants you to determine how we can use this sodium chlorate to generate oxygen. What process should the WNU nanorobots carry out on planet Femto?

CHAPTER 7

PALAEONTOLOGIST

A palaeontologist studies fossils to learn about life as it existed many millions of years ago. Can you name some of the creatures that roamed the Earth during that time? Dinosaurs, you say? That's correct! What can be more exciting than spending the rest of your life studying how dinosaurs lived and died, what they ate, how many kinds of dinosaurs there were or even discovering the remains of new kinds of dinosaurs? Would you be as interested in learning about the other life forms that existed billions of years ago, say, for example, plants and fungi, pollen and spores? What about the study of prehistoric humans? Would you engage in such research purely for the sake of expanding the boundaries of human knowledge? Or would you seek to apply such knowledge to solve present-day problems? Whatever your preference, palaeontology covers all this and more.

Conventionally, it is subdivided into nine different streams:

1. **Micropalaeontology:** Study of microfossils, that is, fossil remains which are between 1 millimetre and 4 millimetres long, irrespective of whether they are bacteria, fungi, plants or animals

2. **Palaeobotany:** Study of fossil plants; this usually includes the study of fossil algae and fungi in addition to land and sea plants

3. **Palynology:** Study of pollen and spores, both living and fossil

4. **Invertebrate palaeontology:** Study of invertebrate animal fossils

5. **Vertebrate palaeontology:** Study of vertebrate fossils, from primitive fishes to mammals but usually not humans

6. **Human palaeontology (also called paleoanthropology):** The study of prehistoric human and protohuman fossils, which among other things helps us in our research on the origins of the human species

7. **Taphonomy:** Study of the processes of formation and preservation of fossils

8. **Ichnology:** Study of fossil tracks, trails and footprints, which is especially significant in the study of larger animals such as dinosaurs

9. **Palaeoecology:** Study of the ecology and climate of the past

You don't have to find a dinosaur in your backyard to become a palaeontologist. But in many ways, palaeontology is more difficult than many other science disciplines like physics, chemistry, biology or geology, because to be a good palaeontologist you must well versed in all these fields. Palaeontology is among the broadest synergy of sciences.

As a palaeontologist, you will not talk in terms of days, hours, minutes and seconds, or even years, decades or centuries. Instead, your everyday vocabulary will include words like eons, eras, periods, epochs and ages, which are units of the geologic timescale that measures the age of the Earth. Within this, the largest unit of time is the supereon, which is made up of eons. Eons are divided into eras. Eras are further divided into periods. Periods are divided into epochs and epochs into ages.

Let us understand this with the exact time spans within which the evolution of the Earth happened. Here are some important milestones in the Earth's lifespan. It would be useful to keep a pen and paper ready with you and keep writing the years to help you understand better.

4550 million years ago (Hadean Eon): The Earth was born, along with the Sun, about 4.55 billion years ago, or bya (4550 million years ago or mya), as a palaeontologist would say. Back then, the Earth was a rapidly spinning dense ball of very hot gases, with little atmosphere, rocky surfaces or water. This is called the Hadean Eon, after the Greek god Hades, who is said to rule hell or the underworld.

According to one theory, about 23 million years after its birth, or circa 4530 mya, the Earth caught hold of a stray celestial body with its force of gravity and the Moon was born. The Moon exerted its own pull on the Earth, thus slowing down the pace of its rotation, making days and nights longer.

4000 million years ago (onset of the Archean Eon): The solar system was formed in the Hadean Eon. For about 500 million years during this time, stray rocks and meteors bombarded the Earth, and new elements from outer space landed on it. This chaotic phase stopped about 4 bya, bringing an end to the Hadean Eon and ushering in the Archean Eon.

3500 million years ago (Archean Eon): Once the massive bombarding stopped, the first form of life appeared on the Earth—the single-celled prokaryotes. Most of these early life forms survived on carbon dioxide and not oxygen. Remember, the atmosphere then had very high temperatures and was full of toxic gases. Around the same time the first form of photosynthesis began pumping small amounts of oxygen into the atmosphere.

2300 million years ago (start of the Proterozoic Eon): The biological activity led to a slow increase in oxygen in the atmosphere for the next 1200 million years, till the atmosphere turned oxygen rich. This happened roughly around 2300 mya, almost at the midpoint of the Earth's current age. Then the existing life forms which survived on carbon dioxide stopped evolving and almost vanished, and new single-celled life forms emerged, which thrived on oxygen.

This transition was a remarkable leap in the evolution of life as we know it. In fact the new single-celled prokaryotes were nothing short of an evolution miracle, and over the next 2000 billion years, these single-celled creatures, less than a nanometre in size, would transform into complex life forms like humans. The Archean Eon ended around this time and the Proterozoic Eon began.

2000 million years ago (Proterozoic Eon): These new prokaryotes quickly evolved in the Proterozoic Eon. They grew better cell organs and a nucleus containing DNA, which helped codify life for the first time. These new life forms, though still single-celled, are called eukaryotes.

1500 million years ago (Proterozoic Eon): Within 500 million years of their existence, eukaryotes were able to form the first sustainable multicellular organism. Now many cells could get together and exchange food and even functions leading to complex life forms, which would eventually start sensing atmosphere.

800 million years ago (Proterozoic Eon): Multicellular organisms kept becoming more complex and larger in size. Towards the end of the Proterozoic Eon, the first form of animals, with more or less

fixed organs, appeared. But these were small invertebrates, which could not move or sense much, like a jellyfish. They lived in water.

542 million years ago (start of the Phanerozoic Eon): The Phanerozoic Eon, which continues till today, started around 542 mya. This was also the time of the Cambrian Explosion, where, in the narrow time window of 20 million years, animals became complex, larger and organized. Plants, too, which were so far confined within oceans, started growing on the Earth by drawing oxygen from the atmosphere and nutrients from the soil. These plants became the first source of food for early land animals.

Remember we had said that eons are divided into eras? The Phanerozoic Eon is divided into three such eras: the Paleozoic, Mesozoic and Cenozoic eras.

380 million years ago (Paleozoic Era): With the availability of plants on land, and hence food, the first land animals appeared. Around this period, there was another evolution—vertebrates appeared on the Earth for the first time.

250 million years ago (Mesozoic Era): The Mesozoic era, which followed the Paleozoic era, is when the dinosaurs evolved.

Remember we said that each era can be further divided into periods? So the Mesozoic era is subdivided into the Triassic, Jurassic and Cretaceous periods. The Mesozoic era recorded rapid development of reptiles. Among the first few species were the crocodiles.

1 - Amphicoelias Fragillimus - 60m
2 - Argentinosaurus Huinculensis - 35m
3 - Mamenchisaurus Sinocanadorum - 35m
4 - Sauroposeidon Proteles - 28m
5 - Supersaurus Vivianae - 33m

In the Triassic Period (from 250 mya to 200 mya) the Archosaurs and Pterosaurs (the flying dinosaurs) originated. Mammals first appeared in this period.

In the Jurassic Period (from 200 mya to 150 mya), huge herbivorous dinosaurs such as sauropods, measuring up to 60 metres in length, appeared. Birds too appeared in this period.

In the Cretaceous Period (150 mya to 70 mya), the well-known T-Rex or Tyrannosaurs appeared on the Earth. At the same time, birds started defeating the flying dinosaurs and began to dominate the skies.

66 million years ago (start of Cenozoic Era): At the end of the Mesozoic Era, around 66 mya, a giant meteor hit the Earth near

modern Mexico. The crater that appeared due to the impact is about 180 kilometres in diameter and 20 kilometres deep. It is believed that this led to the end of the dinosaurs. This also marks the start of the Cenozoic Era of geology history.

The Cenozoic Era is divided into three periods.

The oldest is the Paleogene period (65 mya to 28 mya), then came the Neogene period (28 mya to 3.6 mya), and finally the current Quaternary period (3.6 mya up to now).

The first apes, horses and modern birds began to appear in the Neogene period.

Remember we said that even a period can be subdivided into smaller epochs, each a few hundred thousand years long?

So the Quaternary period is divided into the Pleistocene epoch (2.5 mya to 1.25 mya) and the Holocene epoch (from about 1.25 mya to now). The Pleistocene epoch saw the appearance of the modern man—the Stone Age is a part of this epoch. The Holocene epoch is our modern time. But even within this epoch, the Sahara transformed into a desert from a grassland.

So, we see how palaeontologists measure time. Can you spot the current time in the words of a palaeontologist? (Hint: Use the eon, era, period and epoch)

Look at the endnote for the answer.

_____

_____

_____

The Future of Palaeontology

Even though palaeontology is a relatively young the Earth science, it has contributed greatly to overturning many established notions about the past. One can expect this trend to continue in the near future as well.

Palaeontology is going to have one very distinct application—predicting the future. It seems odd that a science dealing with history can be equally useful to predict the future. But the truth is that a close study of geological time may also contain solutions to many of our environmental and conservation issues. As we know, the Earth, and life on it, has not been stable through time and change is always happening. It is quite likely that potential future situations have happened earlier, for instance, the effect of variation concentration of carbon dioxide. Again, only palaeontologists will be able to predict such things.

Palaeontology is also expected to make breakthrough discoveries in another area which will probably be even more important: that of understanding microorganisms better. Palaeontology has explained how certain bacteria and other microorganisms went extinct, and due to what external factors. These will soon be documented and, in the future, such a database can be extremely useful to defeat the pandemic spreading mutation of microorganisms, similar to those that are already documented. This would be a convergence between palaeontology and medical sciences.

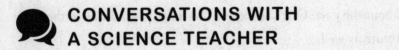

CONVERSATIONS WITH A SCIENCE TEACHER

What are fossils?

'Fossil' refers to the physical evidence of former life in the period of time before recorded human history. Fossils may include remains of living organisms, impressions of their physical form on rocks, and marks created in sediments by their movement.

There is no uniformly agreed age at which such evidence can be termed fossilized. But it is broadly understood that anything more than a few thousand years can be considered a fossil. These may include the near past, such as prehistoric humans, or very old forms like dinosaurs.

The earliest reported fossil discoveries date from 3.5 bya, just around the Great Oxidation event. However, it wasn't until approximately 600 mya that multicellular life began to enter the fossil record. Hence, most of the hunt for fossils is directed after this period.

Not all dead bodies of plants and animals become fossils. It is a chain of some very special events that enable fossilization. It needs rapid and permanent burial, thereby protecting the specimen from all kinds of environmental or biological disturbance. It also needs oxygen deprivation, which limits decay; then it needs continued sediment accumulation as opposed to an eroding surface, ensuring the fossil remains buried in the long term; and the absence of excessive heating, cooling or compression which might otherwise destroy the fossil. Most fossils occur inside.

How do we find out the age of fossils?

Today's knowledge of fossil ages comes primarily from radiometric dating, also known as radioactive dating. Such dating relies on the properties of isotopes or variants of the same chemical element. Isotopes are identical to the element in all but one key feature—the number of neutrons inside their nucleus, which is the core of the atom.

Usually, atoms of the same element contain an equal number of protons and neutrons. If there are too many or too few neutrons, the atom is unstable and sheds the excess proton or neutron particles until its nucleus reaches a stable state.

Imagine the nucleus as a pyramid of building blocks. Now, if you try to add extra blocks to the sides of the pyramid, they may remain balanced for a while, but they'll eventually fall away and leave behind a stable structure. The same is true if you take a block away from one of the pyramid's sides. Eventually, some of the blocks will fall away, leaving a smaller, more durable structure.

In case of the pyramid of elements, or isotopes, the time taken for unstable structures to become stable varies from element to element. The result is like a 'radioactive clock' that ticks away as unstable isotopes decay into stable ones. You cannot predict exactly when a specific unstable atom, or parent, will decay into a stable atom. But you can predict how long it will take a large group of atoms to decay. The element's half-life is the amount of time it takes for half the parent atoms in a sample to become 'daughters'.

To read the time on this radioactive clock, scientists use a device called a mass spectrometer to measure the number of parent (unstable) and daughter (stable) atoms. The ratio of parents to daughters can tell the researcher how old the specimen is. The more parent isotopes there are—and the fewer daughter isotopes—the younger the sample would be. The half-life of the isotope being measured determines how useful it is at dating very old samples. Once all the parents have become daughters, there's no more basis for comparison between the two isotopes.

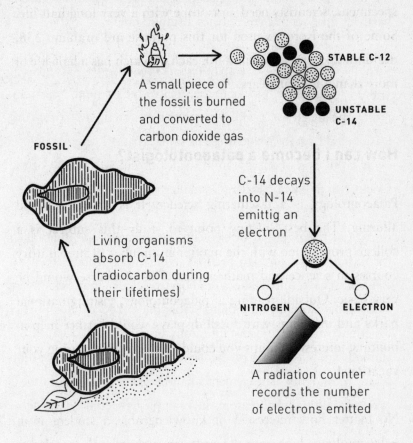

A small piece of the fossil is burned and converted to carbon dioxide gas

STABLE C-12

UNSTABLE C-14

FOSSIL

C-14 decays into N-14 emittig an electron

Living organisms absorb C-14 (radiocarbon during their lifetimes)

NITROGEN   ELECTRON

A radiation counter records the number of electrons emitted

The most widely known form of radiometric dating is carbon-14 dating. This is what archaeologists use to determine the age of man-made samples such as Stone Age tools. But carbon-14 dating won't work on dinosaur fossils. The half-life of carbon-14 is about 6000 years, so carbon-14 dating is only effective on samples that are less than 50,000 years old. Dinosaur bones, on the other hand, are millions of years old; some fossils are billions of years old. To determine the ages of these specimens, scientists need an isotope with a very long half-life. Some of the isotopes used for this purpose are uranium-238, uranium-235 and potassium-40, each of which has a half-life of more than a million years.

How can I become a palaeontologist?

Palaeontology is a fascinating science. It is mysterious and alluring. The best starting point to study this subject is a college programme with the maximum number of preparatory courses in science and mathematics. This of course would be very basic. Outside reading in palaeontology, visiting national parks and museums with fossil displays would further help in building interest. Perhaps you could even join a dig during your vacations!

No matter how interested or knowledgeable a student is in palaeontology, high overall grades in high school are almost always required for admission to a good college or university, which is a necessary prerequisite for a career in palaeontology.

We would suggest choosing an undergraduate institution having quality teaching and learning modules in general science education, especially biology and geology programmes. At this stage the student has to make the complicated decision of choosing what course to opt for, biology or geology. The ideal arrangement is a double-major, with full undergraduate training in both the fields.

Now, various universities have different strengths in different areas, depending on the faculty and the specialization of the researchers working in them. You can probably find the ones interesting to you by reading their published papers in various professional journals such as the *Journal of Palaeontology*, *Palaeobiology*, *American Palaeontologist*, *Palaios* and *Geology*. Make an effort to contact professors and request to visit their facilities. We assure you, you will get to see a lot more interesting stuff and facts which will also help you learn more about their graduate programmes. This might also impress the academics, once they are convinced of your willingness to know more about that particular field.

 MEET THE EXPERT

Dr Ashok Sahni obtained his Masters in geology (1963) from Lucknow University and PhD (geology) (1968) from the University of Minnesota, USA. He was a Humboldt Research Fellow, Institute for Palaeontology at the University of Bonn (1977, 1983), and Professor of Palaeobiology and In-charge, Scanning Electron Microscope Facilities and Senior Scientist, INSA (Indian National Science Academy), Centre of Advanced Study in Geology, Panjab University, Chandigarh (1979–2009). He is still associated with Panjab University, Chandigarh as an Emeritus Professor. Professor Sahni has been closely involved in the popularization of science and setting up of museums and natural history parks. He has also served on the INSA Council.

His work in paleontology and related fields is famed across the world and he has extensively worked on early mammalian evolution and dinosaurian diversity. He was instrumental in placing India on the global dinosaur map when he and his team put together the fossils of *Rajasaurus narmadensis*—India's nine-metre-high carnivorous dinosaur. He has authored over 200 publications.

Q. Please tell us about the kind of work you do in the field of paleontology.

Palaeontology or the science of fossils is for all those who are interested in exploring the Earth for the secrets that now lie buried in rock in the form of plant and animal remains. My interest in the field was sparked by the numerous trips to the Himalayas with my father as a child. He showed me fossils in rocks: shells, fossil bones, leaves, petrified tree trunks. He was a palaeontologist, one who studies animal fossils, while his elder brother, Birbal Sahni, was a palaeobotanist, someone who studies fossil plants. It was therefore quite natural for me to get interested in the subject. In 1963, as an eager twenty-two-year-old, I left India to do a PhD in palaeontology from the USA. My research was centred in the badlands of Montana where some of the iconic Cretaceous dinosaur fossils had been discovered.

As paleontologists, we go with a team of workers to localities where rocks of our interest are exposed. We collect fossils noting carefully the sedimentary environments in which these have been found. Returning to our laboratory, we then identify the fossils and try to build a picture of how life existed in the past. Our focus can range widely: from the spatial position of India several hundred million years ago to specific questions related to whether the fossil forms lived in a tidal zone, in an estuary or in a delta.

Q. What motivated you to take up a career in this field? When were you first inspired to be a palaeontologist?

My greatest inspiration in my chosen career is the joy and thrill of coming across a new fossil. That moment is special and precious! When my students and I found dinosaur eggs and nests in the city of Jabalpur more than thirty years ago, we all became so excited that one of my students went back to the site with a torch in his hand and worked late into the night, much to our concern! My love for palaeontology lies in the fact that I love to travel, unravel the secrets of the Earth by visiting rock exposures and use my scientific knowledge and experience to make interpretations of the age of the rocks, the ancient environment in which these life forms lived and how climates have changed throughout the history of the Earth. I can therefore combine my interest in the Earth and my love for exploration into a viable science that I find very satisfying.

Q. What do you think is the future of palaeontology and associated sciences? Do you see their application in exploration for outer space some day?

Palaeontology has a very bright future: here are some of the fields that are going to benefit from the study of fossils and palaeontology.

  a. Biomechanics: This is a field that has immense potential for engineering applications. It studies the physical ways in which animals and plants deal with their environments or have dealt with the physical world in the past. For example ever since life originated some 3.4 billion (3.4 x 10^9) years ago, myriad life forms have evolved as they struggled to subdue the forces of gravity on land and in the depths of oceans. The challenge was to sustain their life processes in special environments. The large dinosaurs, some of whom attained 60 to 70 tons in weight, are good examples of gravity-bearing structures, and the giant flying reptiles with a wingspan of nearly 10 metres exemplify the first experiments in aerodynamics. What is more remarkable is the fact that their skeletons are made of nanometre-sized crystallites of the bio-mineral apatite (hydroxy calcium phosphate). Similarly, by studying micrometre-sized planktonic organisms in oceans and in lakes, scientists can learn a lot about their structure and apply this data to nanotechnology.

b. Climate change: As our physical world is in perpetual motion, change, including climate change, has been a constant feature. The biological world has contributed greatly to this change. One of the most remarkable upheavals on the Earth was the Great Oxidation Event some 2.2 billion years ago, when photosynthesis increased the amount of oxygen in our atmosphere. This allowed for the evolution of higher life forms, including the advent of man. Fossils are one of the keys in deciphering the climates of the past and predicting future climatic events.

c. Astrobiology: As mankind's discoveries of interstellar space continue, we are bound to discover signs of life in other planets that have water similar to that found on Earth. In such cases, studies of fossils that existed on early the Earth will be invaluable in understanding the environmental conditions on other cosmic bodies. In fact we can find special environments in which life exists. For example, 'Black Smokers' are sulphide-rich vents in deep oceanic waters that promote the existence of special forms of life where oxygen is lacking. Such studies are essential in understanding the evolution of life under special conditions.

d. Survivorship of some life forms and the extinction of others: In the great cycle of life, fossils have a great story to tell. The lowly cockroach and the crocodile have survived the earth-shaking catastrophes while other, more complex organisms have fallen by the wayside and become extinct. In order to build a better tomorrow, scientists can learn some basic principles of survivorship from all organisms past and present in order to develop their strategy in longevity and coping with adversity.

Q. What is your message to the young people who are aspiring to take up a career in palaeontology?

Palaeontology offers you a pathway to learn from the Earth, visit exotic rock exposures, collect fossils and then interpret their secrets in a scientific manner. Your research will have a lasting contribution both on basic and applied sciences and will be personally fulfilling—so follow your dreams.

 NOTE TO PARENTS

Of the 4.5 billion years of the Earth's existence, we only know about the last 100 million years—less than 3 per cent of its life. In the future, by using better radio-dating and deploying a wider variety of fossils and samples, palaeontologists will be able to study in depth about the Earth's past. By studying the events of the past, and their causes, palaeontologists are expected to help predict future events and work on mitigation strategies against disasters.

Palaeontology is a very advanced and dedicated stream, and hence a high level of education is needed. Moreover, palaeontology is a resource-intensive field, often involving digging large tracts of land or ocean in remote areas and using sophisticated instruments, so only the best and very resource-rich universities conduct such courses. There are very few qualified palaeontologists available globally and hence they are in great demand by government institutions across the world, international organizations and academic institutions.

OATH FOR THE ASPIRING PALAEONTOLOGIST

'As a great palaeontologist, I will be remembered for finding new realities about the evolution of the planet and its life forms, and hence contributing in developing a strategy by which humankind can be better prepared to handle any future terrestrial or outer space event which may affect life on Earth.'

(Write this oath in the space below. You can also add new thoughts and goals for yourself as a palaeontologist.)

_____

_____

_____

_____

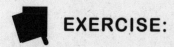

EXERCISE:

This exercise requires an Internet connection or access to a library. Here is a list of different events in the Earth's history:

1. Formation of grasslands
2. Closing of the gap between North and South America and the formation of Isthmus of Panama
3. Snowball Earth, when the ice sheets reached even the equator

As a future palaeontologist, you are required to find the time stamp of these eons, eras, periods and epochs. In some cases, you may be able to find only some of the parameters, so leave the corresponding values blank. Fill in the following table:

	EON	ERA	PERIOD	EPOCH
FORMATION OF GRASSLANDS				
FORMATION OF ISTHMUS OF PANAMA				
SNOWBALL EARTH				

1 Answer: We are in the Phanerozoic Eon, Cenozoic Era, Quaternary Period and Holocene Epoch.

ACKNOWLEDGEMENTS

In writing this book, our ideas and ideas have evolved through the interactions we have had with a number of students, teachers, professors and other people from across India and even in other nations we have visited.

A large portion of the thoughts expressed in this book are essentially extensions of dreams, imaginings, perils, ambitions, hopes and challenges of all these people, especially the youth. These thoughts revolve around some of the futuristic pathways which science will open. At many points we have also captured their concerns for the future of humankind and linked them with how science, good science, can address them. We thank all these stakeholders, friends and acquaintances, some even strangers, and the young community, who have openly shared their views and thoughts, which have taken shape in this book. We sincerely hope that our book captures their ingenious thoughts.

We would like to express our gratitude especially to the expert contributors of this book—Professor Sethu Vijayakumar, Professor Ashok Sahni, Dr Jogi Pattisapu and Dr Ashok Patil, who helped us with the expert sections and also with many other ideas which shaped the content of the book. We are also thankful to Professor Sahni for his help with the pictures of his work on palaeontology.

We would like to thank Ms Sohini Mitra, Ms Jaishree Ram Mohan and Ms Nimmy Chacko for helping us with the editing and quality improvement of the content. We also thank Ms Kashmira Sarode for her excellent work with the illustrations, Ms Pia Alize Hazarika for the cover and Ms Piya Kapur for all the marketing support. We thank Mr Jayraj Pandya, Mr Saurav, Ms Meenal Ajmera and Ms Nishtha for their help in reviewing and research.

We also sincerely acknowledge the contribution of Mr Udayan Mitra and Ms Hemali Sodhi from Penguin for their excellent support in bringing out this book in good time.

We also express our acknowledgement and sincere gratitude to Shri Harry Sheridon, Shri R.K. Prasad and Shri Dhanshyam Sharma for their untiring help towards putting this book together.

A.P.J. Abdul Kalam and Srijan Pal Singh

Authors

Image Credits

1. Srijan Pal Singh
2. Srijan Pal Singh
3. Getty Images
4. DARPA
5. Getty Images
6. Getty Images
7. Getty Images
8. Getty Images
9. Kashmira Sarode
10. Getty Images
11. Getty Images
12. Dr A.P.J. Abdul Kalam
13. Kashmira Sarode
14. Getty Images
15. Getty Images
16. Dr Ashok Sahni
17. Dr Ashok Sahni